Letters to My *Lord*

Intimate Conversations with Christ

Letters *to My* *Lord*

Intimate Conversations with Christ

Daniel A. Lord, S.J.

Christian Classics ❦ Notre Dame, Indiana

Nihil obstat: Brendan W. Lawlor, Censor Deputatus

Imprimatur: ✠ Robert F. Joyce, Bishop of Burlington

June 9, 1969

Founded in 1865, Ave Maria Press is a ministry of the United States Province of Holy Cross.

www.christian-classics.com

Paperback: ISBN-13 978-0-87061-300-5

Cover image © Godong / robertharding.

Cover and text design by Christopher D. Tobin.

Printed and bound in the United States of America.

Library of Congress Cataloging-in-Publication Data is available

Contents

Editor's Note by Thomas Gavin, S.J. ix

Foreword by Michael Rossmann, S.J. xi

Introduction by David J. Endres xiii

I 1

II 9

III 17

IV 23

V 31

VI 39

VII 45

VIII 51

IX 59

X 65

XI 71

XII 79

XIII 85

XIV 91

XV 97

XVI 101

Epilogue: Cancer Is My Friend 108

Editor's Note

Thomas Gavin, S.J.

Have you ever looked cancer in the eye? I would like to introduce you to a man who looked it in the eye and stared it down. A few months after he was told by his doctors that he had cancer of both lungs, Father Daniel Lord wrote an article which was copied in magazines and newspapers throughout the United States and Canada. In it he said,

> When the verdict was cancer, I was relieved. I had expected to die some day of heart trouble or a stroke, and I dreaded the sudden and perhaps sacrament-less death. Cancer seemed kindly. I liked the gentle warning. In a sudden spurt of energy and a determination to use time to the best advantage, I found I was itching to write some of those books that I had long planned. Then I hit the road, back at my routine of talks and meetings and play rehearsals. So often have I taught the faith to others that, of a sudden, I found my friend, cancer, teaching the faith to me. The realization that one has cancer sharpens one's whole outlook on life; the earth is more beautiful, the sky a little clearer, and every moment of the day precious, a thing to be hoarded.

While doing research for a biography of Father Lord, I came across an intimate, personal document that he wrote in a St. Louis hospital during his last retreat. On the second day of his retreat he was told that he had terminal cancer. He called this document *Letters to My Lord*, and that is exactly what they are—casual, intimate letters which spring from a deep faith and show an easy familiarity with the life of the spirit. The letters are a brief synopsis of his attitudes on life set in a framework of the *Spiritual Exercises* of St. Ignatius. But nowhere is there a reference to his fatal disease, nowhere a trace of bitterness or resentment.

This book, Father Lord's last, is his spiritual testament: a lyric on the many things that he loved, and a vow that even in his last days he had much work to begin. It is an affirmation of life—life here on earth and life everlasting—in the face of death. We are his heirs and debtors for having been left so rich and genial a vision of that kingdom to which we are all invited.

Foreword

Michael Rossmann, S.J.

When I first heard about Father Daniel Lord, he seemed like he was from another planet. Like Lord, I'm an American Jesuit and do a lot of writing directed at my fellow young people. That being said, when I first heard about his leadership of the Sodality of the Blessed Virgin Mary and the lyrics of its theme song—"An army of youth flying the standards of Truth. . . . Heads lifted high, Catholic Action our cry"—I could not help but think, "Good luck trying that at a high school or college today!" The issues affecting young people in the Catholic Church today seemed so far removed from those of the first half of the twentieth century that it was easy to dismiss much work from that era, even from someone as popular as Daniel Lord.

Thank God I found this book. As I sit with his spiritual writings, I am amazed at how profoundly relevant Daniel Lord is for our times. Some of his language can seem old-fashioned, but the core messages are as timely today as they were when he wrote them just before his death in 1955.

Perhaps that's not so surprising. Through these intimate letters written to Christ, we discover that the wellspring of Lord's indefatigable writing, directing, and organizing was the perennial truth and joy of the Gospel. In one letter, Lord writes, "For human problems are basically endlessly repetitious and embarrassingly simple. The answers you gave to an audience almost twenty hundred years ago sound strangely modern today" (see page 75). Like the Gospel message itself, Lord's writings are similarly "strangely modern."

I'm convinced that nothing is more attractive than joy. We may disagree about politics. We may have different tastes in friends or film or food. We may have had different or even difficult experiences of the Church. But joy is attractive. Joy is contagious. Joy can unite those who may not be united by much else.

That being said, as I talk with my fellow young adults and reflect on my own experience, we are often uncertain about how to actually find joy. In reading *Letters to My Lord*, however, the fog of uncertainty burns away. While there may not be a neat and tidy formula for happiness, Lord's writings make it inescapably clear that gratitude is part of the equation.

He is quick to point to his faults—which seem like molehills compared to my mountains—and is almost never self-congratulatory. He does make one positive statement about himself, however. He writes, "At least, I am grateful" (see page 15). Talk about an understatement! Gratitude pours off the page again and again in these letters written during the same week he received his cancer diagnosis. Lord does not simply feel grateful; he *practices* gratitude. A grateful man is a happy man, and Lord was a paragon of both.

As popular as Lord was in his day, simply recreating the organizations he led or restaging the musicals he directed probably would not work in our context. Some of his popular writing is tied so much to his own era that it would not be as accessible to the contemporary reader. Here in these letters, however, we are given a glimpse of a man on fire with his relationship with Christ—a relationship, as Lord demonstrates, that is just as accessible to each one of us. It doesn't sound stuffy; it doesn't even sound particularly churchy. It sounds authentic.

As different as Lord's time can seem, the eternal questions he raises and the relationship with Christ that he models are as relevant as ever. We are still yearning for joy. Reflecting on these letters makes it abundantly clear that Father Daniel Lord had joy and that he offers us a path to it today.

Introduction

David J. Endres

Daniel A. Lord, S.J. (1888–1955), was among the best-known American Jesuits of the twentieth century. Catholics who came of age, in particular, during the interwar years were undoubtedly influenced by Lord's work. His roles included directing the national Sodality of Our Lady and editing its popular magazine, *The Queen's Work*, authoring hundreds of literary and dramatic works, founding the intensive training program called Summer Schools of Catholic Action, and leading the effort to safeguard Americans from immoral films. Born in Chicago, Lord attended Catholic schools throughout his elementary and high school years before beginning studies at St. Ignatius College, Chicago. It was there that he became intrigued by the life of St. Francis Xavier and attracted to life as a Jesuit. He entered the Society of Jesus in 1909 and was ordained to the priesthood after more than a decade of preparation.

Lord remains an intriguing personality in part because of the divergent assessments of his life and ministry. Not always welcomed nor respected, Lord's fiercest opposition came from the film industry where he was seen as a meddlesome priest set on ruining Hollywood. Similarly, Lord was not always appreciated within the Church or by his confreres. Among the Society of Jesus's band of teachers and scholars, Lord was sometimes viewed as a "popularizer" who exhibited an anti-intellectual approach to the faith. Some considered his use of drama and the mass media to communicate the faith a less than noble means to teach "serious" truths. Due to his specialized work, Lord's ministry often necessitated frequent travel from diocese to diocese, causing him to appear at times as a renegade Jesuit and leading to the assertion by one American bishop that Lord was an example of the harm that could be done when a priest's ministry passed outside the control of the bishops.

These assessments of Lord's life and ministry should not, however, be viewed apart from his remarkable popularity as youth organizer, author, playwright, and media consultant. In particular, his wide appeal among youth, long before the days of recognized "youth ministry," was without parallel. Lord's dramatic and literary works testified to the enduring appeal of themes of heroism, virtue, and faith and their ability to speak to youth in every generation. During his lifetime he successfully energized and engaged hundreds of thousands by employing music, drama, narrative, and ritual as an invitation to spiritual growth.

An Army of Youth

Shortly after his ordination, Lord somewhat unwillingly commenced the work that would frame nearly his entire ministry, becoming director of the Jesuit-sponsored Sodality of the Blessed Virgin Mary. The sodality, which began as a loose network of student-based charitable and devotional groups often headquartered at Jesuit educational institutions, expanded dramatically under Lord's leadership, claiming over two million members at its highpoint. The sodality was labeled a "dying organization" before his involvement, but Lord quickly set to work on a national plan for expansion, beginning with a revival of the sodality's magazine, *The Queen's Work*. The magazine grew to become a major tool for catechesis and evangelization.

Lord's creativity enveloped every aspect of the sodality and Catholic Action movements. Of particular importance was his founding in 1931 of the Summer Schools of Catholic Action, a formational program held in various American cities each summer to train young Catholics to answer the challenge of living out their faith in the modern world. Lord is also remembered for composing the Catholic Action theme song, "For Christ the King," which began,

"An army of youth flying the standards of Truth, We're fighting for Christ the Lord. Heads lifted high, Catholic Action our cry, And the Cross our only sword." Many Catholics educated near mid-century can still recall the tune and its lyrics. Remaining as national director of the sodality until 1948, Lord was the chief architect of the sodality's growth, the organizational and creative force behind what at one time was the most significant movement of American Catholic youth.

Eight Million Words

Noted for his organizing zeal, Lord was also one of the principal participants in the Catholic literary revival of the early twentieth century, aimed at propagating distinctively Catholic literary and dramatic works. Unlike most of his Jesuit counterparts who were attracted to a scholastic, intellectual means of handing on the faith, Lord utilized a popular approach that relied on catchy titles, poems, cartoons, and songs—one that appealed to youth by way of emotion rather than strictly intellect. To this end, Lord began authoring numerous pamphlets and articles driving home the typical themes of "Catholic Action": eucharistic and Marian devotion, modesty in dress and conduct, respect for the family and persons of authority, anti-secularism, and later attacks on the chief "ism": anticommunism. His writings often had provocative titles meant to capture the attention of young people, including *The Church Is a Failure* (1939), *Confession Is a Joy* (1933), and *Don't Marry a Catholic* (1952).

His fresh style won him many followers who had only to look to their parish's literature rack for the latest installments from Lord. Not including letters, it is estimated that he penned an average of twenty thousand words per month over the course of his thirty-five-year ministry, totaling at least eight million words. By the time of his death, Lord had written ninety books, nearly three hundred pamphlets, and countless articles. Dealing with a wide range of contemporary themes, many of Lord's works promoted a proper understanding of human sexuality, the beauty of marriage and family life, and the importance of cultivating priestly and religious vocations. His works had sold more than 25 million copies by the 1960s, assuring that Lord influenced most American Catholics educated in the first half of the twentieth century.

King of Drama

In addition to his literary output, Lord was known for creating and directing elaborate pageants, often with hundreds of participants. An accomplished pianist and teacher of drama, he authored fifty-eight musicals. Relying on local talent with minimal rehearsing, his "musical masques" blended moral and social lessons with historical themes, often featuring the triumphant medieval crusader as the protagonist. Historian Peter McDonough has called Lord's pageants "the multimedia events of the era" which included "Lord pounding away at the piano, spotlights turning from one end of the proscenium to the other, and much flapping of drapery and theatrical gowns" (*Men Astutely Trained*, 86). Lord took his pageants on the road, from city to city, directing his plays before sold-out venues.

Lord's interest in drama easily transferred into a fascination with film. He earned a reputation as the Catholic authority on film after serving as a consultant to Cecil B. DeMille's *The King of Kings* (1927), a cinematic portrayal of the life of Christ. Within a few years, Lord became prominent in the effort to censor the content of movies as backer of the National Legion of Decency and author of the Motion Picture Production Code. Though he himself was an entertainer who skillfully utilized the stage, Lord's support of film censorship indicated his unwillingness to allow artistic freedom to trump acceptable moral parameters. His involvement in the drafting of the production code remains of particular interest among historians and sociologists, perhaps because it is here that Lord's influence seems most foreign to our contemporary understanding.

Embracing Life in Illness

When in early 1954, at the age of sixty-five, he was diagnosed with lung cancer, Lord asked his doctors, "How long do you think I have? I have very much to do." During his last nine months of life, he worked on several final projects, including reflections from his last retreat, a work that would be titled *Letters to My Lord*, and his autobiography, a self-described "medley of memories" published as *Played by Ear*. Amazingly, after his diagnosis, in the span of three weeks, he wrote four hundred pages and when too weak to write, he spoke into a voice recorder, providing the material to keep two stenographers constantly busy. In his final months, Lord directed one final drama—the 1,200 person production "Joy for the World" performed in Toronto to commemorate the Marian Year.

Lord's embrace of life after his diagnosis evidenced not only a new urgency but also perhaps a refined perspective toward life. This is seen in a letter composed shortly before his death written to a young Trappist monk. Lord offered simple spiritual insights, including, "Keep your eyes on God, and stay close to Him, and let Him do the worrying about you." Lord ended the letter with this final exhortation: "Grow! When you stop growing spiritually, you are asleep or dead."

Father Lord's Legacy

Father Lord's is a life worth remembering, not only because he was one of the most notable Jesuits of the last century, but because he represents a pioneering vision for the Church's ongoing, but especially urgent, work of evangelization. Lord championed a form of public Catholicism meant to compel believers to take their faith out into the world, not to leave it sequestered in churches and schools "safe" for the spread of religion. What appealed to a generation of

Catholics, and what should elicit our admiration today, is Lord's zeal in encountering people through the most effective means available whether through the stage, the written word, or the cinema, employing modern technology and cultural themes without shortchanging the vitality of the Church's teachings.

His literary, dramatic, and organizational contributions, however, should not be viewed in insolation from his own life of faith. His prodigious output was born out of his relationship with the Lord, one of trust and intimacy. His keen spiritual insights, sharpened through suffering and illness, as seen in these pages of *Letters to My Lord* offer a window into his soul. They witness to his relationship to Jesus and his belief in the paschal mystery, not abstractly, but as personally and profoundly connected to his life. These last reflections form a fitting spiritual legacy for Father Lord as he would have wished to have been remembered, one would suspect, less for what he did, than for who he was: a priest, a Jesuit, and a companion of the Lord in life, death, and in the hope of sharing in his resurrection.

I

Dear Lord,

Today I begin my retreat.

Surely this is no news to you. (May I pause here to wonder if you prefer us to write "You" with a capital or a small "Y"? Everyone seems to be divided nowadays—printers and editors and typesetters, I mean—over whether in speaking of you in the third person, to write the pronoun He or he, His and Him or his and him. For years I paid you the willing tribute of capitals. Yet recently a very great life of your Son, published by a great Catholic firm and authored by a holy and learned priest, spelled the pronouns always in lower case. Shall I be permitted to follow his example? Thank you, Lord!)

At any rate, it is not news to you that I have this morning begun my annual retreat. I am making it in St. John's Hospital, St. Louis, where you have graciously allowed me to undergo a physical trial in the midst of your customary lavish care and the charity of the wonderful Sisters of Mercy. They must be very dear to you, as surely they are to me.

With a slight pretense of humor, I have often spoken of a retreat as submergence. "I am submerging this evening," I write in mild facetiousness to friends. And at the end, "Once more I emerge." Would that it had meant that I had sunk into the ocean of your Presence, allowing myself to sense and feel that in you I am living, moving, and possessing my being. I am afraid that it had instead often enough been in a sort of coma. I have put the arms of parentheses around eight days of my life and devoted them to a saint surely not registered in Heaven's guestbook—St. Inertia.

So, though it is not news to you that I am in retreat, it may be a surprise to the angels that this year I intend to keep in close touch with you.

Often enough in times past, the start of a retreat must have seemed almost a severing of connections with my personal Recording Angel . . . at least on the credit side.

I have sometimes wondered why. Prayer, I have told thousands of others, is simply easy conversation with the One who loves us. And surely it should be easy to talk with One who loves and is Love. Yet it remains a fact that prayer is not easy, is it, Lord? Is it hard because it often seems so one-sided? You answer with grace but not with audible replies. And sometimes words are what we want; words that say "Yes," "Certainly," "I have heard you," "Go on, I'm listening."

In response to our prayer, you are extravagant with your gifts. But we are so human; and the reply is what we crave. "Lord, I love you," we say; and though the whole world is the outpouring of your love, we strain for the whisper that says, "I love you, too." "I am sorry that I have done so badly," we confess; and the voice of your priest comes with the comforting assurance that we may go in peace for our sins are forgiven. Now if an overtone to the priestly voice were your sigh of pitying forgiveness, what a difference we would . . . feel.

Yes, I know that "feel" is a poor and unsatisfactory word. But you made us creatures of feeling and surely you are not surprised when we feel sharply the need to hear your voice replying to ours.

This, I recognize, is all self-excuse and lazy demanding. Even in prayer, our conversation with you, you assure us that "my grace is sufficient for you." But even Job the patient found more joy in your voice speaking to him from the whirlwind than from all your other gifts.

At any rate, this time I am writing to you. Do you mind?

I should like to write a letter to my Lord.

I am not quite sure whether a letter is a self-centered sort of thing or a contented sort of thing. But at least it does not expect an immediate answer. When one writes, he writes because he wants to talk to a friend. He cannot reach that beloved person with the throw of his voice, so out from his heart through his fingers pour the thoughts he would like to share. He signs and seals, and sends, and then waits with practiced patience in a world of fairly bad correspondents for his answer. And when the answer comes, the friend have may totally neglected the questions he was asked, have failed to discuss the problems that inspired the first letter, and talks instead about things which interest him. Who cares?

The joy of writing letters is the letters themselves. The answer when it comes is like an almost completely separate and distinct joy. The original writer by that time may have almost forgotten what he wrote about. If the answerer is not careful to repeat the question, taking it for granted that the writer remembers what he wrote, his answer may not make sense.

"Regarding your problem, I'd say, 'Don't worry about it in the least.'"

"What problem?" puzzles the man who posed it in the first letter.

"Your question should be answered with a prompt 'Yes.'"

"What question?" the writer wonders.

Actually it may well have been that by the bare statement of the problem, the problem disappeared; and once the question was asked, the question was already answered. Letters are probably much less for the information of the receiver than for the relief of the writer. Surely it is better to write letters than to receive them.

As you well know, either the nature which you gave me or the training which you afforded me has made me one of the world's most prolific letter writers. As with everything else that I do, I sincerely hesitate to mention the quality of my letters. There is no mistaking the volume. I reach for a typewriter where more modern men reach for a telephone. I am afraid that often enough I have annoyed my associates by sending them a note or letter when a few steps down a corridor might have brought us face to face for what men like to call "a chat." With years, I find it easier to talk to a thousand people and harder to talk to one. In a large audience, one misses the boredom that may be filming the eyes of the individual on whom our conversation is inflicted.

And I surely find it vastly easier to write a letter than make an oral explanation, to solve a problem by mail than to handle it face to face.

A lot of elements that you understand much better than I, dear Lord, enter into that. They say that the English find it hard to talk out their inner emotions; yet Heaven knows they are among the world's great and fluent writers. And there is English in my ancestry. But isn't that just as true of the sometimes garrulous Irish? An Irishman can tell a wonderful yarn or sing the endless stanzas of an Irish ballad; yet in the heart of his family he may often be a silent, almost brooding fellow. The great love in his heart for his wife seldom seems to find expression in what we call "pretty speeches," though he may write her a great poem or a lovely song. He's proud of his children and often at a loss how to tell them. He can shout out amusing nothings in a crowd of strangers and sit silently over a pipe and a mug with a friend. And there is much of the Irish in my veins.

For the English and the Irish in me, dear Lord, an unaccustomed thanks. I have not thanked you before for ancestry. Now, without disparagement of any of the splendid nationalities on earth, I am grateful to you for long American tradition, for what the English ancestors of my father and the Irish forebears of my mother gave me. I could wish that I were even more a "mongrel," with more of the traditions of your races and nations, your children across the earth, furnishing me the raw material of my character.

At any rate, I have, thanks to your goodness, found writing letters a pleasant privilege and an inspiring duty.

I have liked answering the strangers whose questions came to me over strange signatures that were never to know an identifying face. I have tried never to let an unanswered letter rest long on my desk. To the relief of my own soul, I have written hundreds, thousands of letters to friends across the world. I have liked to share the joys and triumphs even of personal strangers with a little note. It has seemed to me a matter of visiting the sick and burying the dead and talking with the prisoner in his cell when I have written in sympathy or tried to write what grief or loss or failure can mean to the enrichment of the human soul. I have not been present for many weddings; my letters have taken my place. I do not often form part of the "wake" around the dead; but I have been there with letters of condolence.

All this you know, dear Lord. Why tell you?

Well, just for the surprising fact that flashed upon me; I have never written you a letter. You are my dearest and best friend, and you have never had so much as a note from me. I have talked about myself in letters to many another friend, and never put on paper to you anything that concerned me. Oh, I have made the jottings that mark the course of a retreat. When some "light" flashed upon me, I noted it down. But that was for myself, not for you.

I have written uncounted letters of thanks, and never one "Thank You" note to my greatest Benefactor. I have written countless letters on the occasions of death and never wrote once to condole with you on the death of your Divine Son. I have hurried into the mail the notes that shared with friends some small success, which, incidentally, I may have mentioned to you in a sudden spurt of prayer. I have confessed by mail my failures and described to my own relief and the sympathy of friends problems that blocked my forward movement, detours that led me far from my goal, mistakes that were sometimes funny and often tragic, collapses which were shameful when I wrote them down and less dreadful once they had been shared. And all this was in letters to friends . . . not in letters to my Lord.

Yet the joy and strength I have known in correspondence— couldn't they be intensified if the correspondent were yourself? ("Yourself" is what the Irish call you sometimes; does it not make you divinely smile?) If I have found talking to friends sometimes hard and writing to them always easy, might I, who find prayer hard, not find letters to you simple and fluent?

Have I missed telling you a great many things you wanted me to tell, simply because I can be diffident about small glories and mighty failures? You have written me the Divine Correspondence which is the Sacred Scripture. So I feel that if I write to you, I can interrupt my writing to pick up your answer and read it in advance. Odd, but correspondence with you would be rather strange; your answering letters were written centuries before my inquiring letters were ever penned. Or is that too human a viewpoint?

So as I begin my retreat, and with your leave, my dear Lord, I shall write to you.

Perhaps letters to you should be masterpieces of epistolary composition. But even as I wrote that collection of polysyllables, I felt your deprecating smile. You wouldn't want me to pause for words, the precise and elegant word, when writing to other friends I let my fingers fly over the portable keyboard? You wouldn't want me to write letters that smack of the classic correspondence of the 1700s when I live in the second half of the exciting, perilous twentieth century?

Actually these are letters from a son in exile.

They are field reports from a minor soldier in an endless siege.

They concern, as topical letters must, the trivialities of the year and the month and the day and the hour.

They are meant less to inform you, who know everything, than to inform myself.

You understand my feelings before I put them down on paper. Perhaps I understand them better because I do. You have given the grace that makes possible some minimal triumphs, yet you might like a report on them. You have watched with regret my wanton smashing of your plans and need no list of causalities. Yet would my apologies ring as true as I want them to read? And would I do less badly another time because I had confessed this time's mistakes to a patient Lord?

So as I think I shall write; and as I write I shall think. And my prayer will be a letter rather than words upon the eloquent air, and the habit of a lifetime can be turned experimentally to the spiritual release of advancing years.

Like a small child attempting a first letter to an affectionate parent, I make blanket apology for mistakes, whatever they may be. I confess that, like all egocentric correspondents, I shall be abnormally dull. I acknowledge in advance that my news is stale, my emotions trivial, my failures inconsequential, my successes unhistoric. Yet my letters come with gratitude and love and a desire to be known, from the heart of

Your grateful son,

II

Dear Lord,

Do you grow a little weary with the way I give good advice to others? Surely you must, for you give so much of everything else and really so little advice. Just a few wise laws, and for the rest, the common sense and judgment which ought to make good advice superfluous. Anyhow, I apologize for the vast quantities of good advice I have handed out over the years, and the little attention I pay to what I am giving others. Probably I am so fascinated with the music of my voice that I don't listen to what my voice is saying. I've heard that sometimes I advise others wisely and well; they would be astonished to learn that I take in so little of my own "wise" counsel.

I've just been thinking as this retreat starts of the time I spent in two successive weeks giving the same piece of advice to boys and young men. In succession, I gave a retreat at a boys' high school and a men's university. And both times, I found myself saying, with great feeling and sincerity:

"Boys, go home and thank your fathers!"

I think I was a little misty-eyed at the time, for I have reached the point where I can grow mightily sentimental about fathers.

Is that the sign of growing up? A sign, at least? And isn't it a little sad to reach my age and still look for signs of growing up? Emotion over mothers seems to be a thing that develops early. What they do for their children is right there for anyone to see and weep tenderly over. Even fathers are part of the chorus that lifts its hymns of praise to mothers.

Meanwhile the fathers themselves . . .

Anyhow, if you'll graciously recall, I told both groups, in words graded, I hope, to the passage of some four years from Junior in high school to Junior in college, "Go home and write Dad a little note.

Tell him you realize what he has done for you and how much you owe him. Mention two or three outstanding acts of unselfishness you can recall. And say, from your heart, 'Thank you, Father.' Poor chap, the surprise may be almost more than his weary constitution can take. He may look at the letters not through a mist of tears but through eyes knocked out of alignment. But he rates it. And it's about time you appreciated your father."

That may prove, too, that I myself, far too late to do much about it, realize one of the greatest of your gifts was the father you sent into my life. So perhaps you are not too surprised that I am a more than ordinarily ungrateful son toward you, my Father in Heaven. For I was a casual, unappreciative, grasping, thoughtless, patronizing son toward the father you gave me on earth.

Fathers are an unthanked class of human society, aren't they? And in that they are very like yourself.

So since I gave that excellent advice to my young men-retreat-ants the other day, I find myself hearing the echo of that advice as I start my own retreat.

"Say thank you to your Father."

And since you long ago took to his grateful reward the father who gave me the devotion of his life-time on earth, I lift my eyes gratefully to you.

"Thank you, Father! Thank you, very much indeed."

Let's see; if I were to start off to enumerate the reasons why I should be grateful, where should I begin? Where should I end? This would not be a letter. It would be the library of world science, the catalogue of the stars, the codex of natural laws, the entire record of your part in human history. It would begin when the empty void began to flow with the seeds of creation, and Chaos was first shaped and ordered according to your divine plan.

You surely know that I am no scientist. What the great minds of the scientific world write in formulae for the initiated few, I read in Large-Letter Primers. I have never peered through the lenses of Palomar and watched space reach out beyond imagining. I have never mathematically figured the speed of a comet, the heat of a sun, the number of stars in a minor solar system, or where that unseen planet moving through outer space will be a million years from now. I just look at the stars and hear my heart singing; I open my arms and let the sun warm me like the hearth fire in a great hall. I nod when I hear the astronomers talk of the heavens, and I grow fuzzy when the physicists assure me that deep in the heart of every atom are planetary systems more wonderful than what I fuzzily see in space.

I could never prove that there are no two violets in the world alike, nor any two snow crystals on a window pane; I just know that you have made the earth a garden and covered the bare earth of winter with incredibly beautiful lace. I can only nod my agreement when a great mathematician says of you, "Whatever else you may say of God, you can say this surely: He is the greatest mathematician of all." I can with amusement watch the artist strut a bit when he has briefly caught and copied some small sector of the beauty with which you have filled the earth and the skies and the manifold recesses of nature. When the cloth manufacturer has finished his finest fabric, he has something that copies the underside of a moss violet, or the less subtle shades of a fungus, or the iridescence of one of your lower forms of sea urchin.

A sculptor carves the flowing grace of an antelope and freezes it in stone; you touch the antelope and its grace becomes the pure dance of rhythm and power. The painter struggles to catch the smile on his model's face, and once it is caught, gains in it an immortality. You fashioned the million faces of mankind mobile in a million smiles—not one face on canvas but the mighty mural of all mankind.

What a Father is mine!

What an incredibly magnificent Father!

We've a homely phrase for a good father of a family; we say, speaking the words with reverence, "He's a good provider."

Shall I take your time and paragraphs of my letter to thank you for being the kind of miraculous provider you are? Where shall we even start . . . with a catalogue of foods . . . or with a listing of drinks . . . with the furs and fabrics and leathers of our clothing . . . with the materials that await the hands of human builders? With the power of falling water or the healing qualities of quinine bark? With the wonderful thing that is human skin or the marvel that lies hidden for centuries in grey (apparently corrupting) mold? Shall I think back over the meals I have eaten, the warmth I have wrapped about me, the fuel that I have burned in furnace and heating plant, the services of steam and wood and iron and electricity?

What need is there to stress the beauty of the ocean and the buoyancy and cleansing power of water? What of the constant chemistry by which the air around me is kept in perfect balance for my lungs, my eyes, and my pores? What of the slavery of the animals to my appetites and needs and even my sports . . . the cow, the work horse, the racer or jumper, the dog at my heels, the cat on my rug, the birds making spring a recurrent symphony, the worms at work ploughing my fields, the bees creating honey while they bear on their bodies the seed germs of rich crops, the fish we eat or prey after for excitement, the untouched richness of the sea's vast stores of food and mineral?

What a Father is mine!

Who is like my Father, except in pale flattering imitation?

Well, dear Lord, at least for this much I can say my sincere thank you! For the moon that binds us safely with the chains of gravity and make the poets sing . . . for the sun that pulls our nourishment from the mud and paints the western sky with apocalyptic glory . . . for insects and cloud and grass and distant planets.

And all this takes form and meaning when I say, "And your son is grateful." He knows the greatness of his Father and this magnificence with which he carved the universe and stocked it with all that makes life rich and varied and exciting and challenging and a foretaste of the infinity of Heaven.

For the limitlessness of the universe is just that, a kind of appetizer for the infinity of Heaven. Our delicious foods are a poor first course compared to your promise of the eternal banquet. Our house of earth cannot stand architectural comparison with the mansions which you have promised for those who are faithful sons and loving daughters.

Sons and daughters . . .

Children of God . . .

Only the constant repetition of those amazing words makes them stale and squeezes them of their meaning.

Actually they are the answer to all human questioning. They are the complete solution of human greatness and human weakness, of human trial and human destiny.

Children we are, dear Lord, thoughtless, carelessly casual children, the spoiled children of a rich and indulgent Father.

This started off to be a letter of praise, dear Lord. As you see it has already slipped out of control. It started to be a letter of thanks from a grateful son to his gracious Father. But when I start to think of you as my Father, the words begin to explode. They race away from me like wild horses. Lacking the power to express your greatness in precise formulae, I find myself reaching for wildly extravagant adjectives. Only the adjectives aren't extravagant. They are simply pale understatements of what you are and what you have done.

I am the stuttering child telling his great attorney-father how well he spoke before the supreme court of the land.

I am the child with paint-smeared cheeks telling his artist-father that he likes the mural which covers the capitol rotunda.

I am the first-grader congratulating his scientist-father on harnessing the power of the atom.

I am the child just learning to hum who says, when he hears his composer-father's symphony, "It's really a nice tune."

Yet, from my heart, I am glad you are my Father. All the universe you made with almost careless perfection—from pool of rock oil to the Milky Way. Yet will they fade and end, returning to the chaos from which you gently guided them.

That will be when they have served your purposes and mine. For these you made for me. These are almost less your world—you do not need them—than they are mine, for whose brief earth-span they form a glorious background. In the perfection of the Trinity, dear Lord, you need neither sun nor electron, neither star nor violet, neither water, nor animals. It was I, your son, for whom all this was made. They are your gifts to me.

They cry out the majesty and beauty and power of the Father to whose arms I run, whose house I serve and love. All his creatures serve me with the slavish obedience and bursting glory that my Father gave them. I am steward of the incredible treasures and resources of the universe. I am manager of my Father's visible estate.

And you are my Father.

I started this letter with eyes raised to thank you. I find that I want to end it on my knees, my head bent in wonder and in the fear that I might look into the noonday sun, the exploding atom, the glory of your countenance, unprepared, and be destroyed.

That anyone so little as I should be the son of anyone so great as you . . . is a mystery of heredity.

That I should take your universe for granted, without interest, without care, without gratitude, is devastating commentary on my character.

That, like an archangel or a seraph, I should be a Son of God, is too vast a dignity, too high an honor, too embarrassing an inheritance.

Especially when I know how I crawl when I should fly, hug the gutter when I should challenge the mountain tops, boast of the trifles I do so badly when my Father does all things perfectly.

At least, I am grateful. At least I am proud of my Father. At least, I can take my own advice to the sons of earth and say to my Father who is in Heaven, "I am grateful. Make me more grateful still."

Your devoted son,

III

Dear Lord,

Among the many things I am not, I am not a botanist.

You did not share with me that creative gift which is called the green thumb. Indeed, as I look back over life's many failures, I find them epitomized in my dealings with green, growing things. There were those radish seeds I planted as a child, and when the green shoots appeared, I pulled them up each day to see how the radish root had developed. You recall that that did not notably help my harvest of radishes that year. A gardener who cannot grow radishes is not much of a gardener, that's for sure.

Obedience set me to the task, as a novice, of transplanting black walnut trees. I transplanted the young trees, doing precisely as I was instructed to do. Or so I thought. One thousand young saplings stood in military formation when I had finished my job. Then, like a regiment doomed by poor command to defeat, all one thousand of them died. Dear Lord, mine has often been a destructively heavy and clumsy hand.

Yet I have an unintelligent love of flowers. When the other day kind friends sent a dozen long-stemmed roses to my sickroom, I was most grateful. I marveled a little that your genius had given us in the same botanical family (or so I think) the apple and the rose.

It is a tribute to you that you fashioned in the rose so beautiful a thing that lovers can sing, "My love is like a red, red rose," and feel that they have paid the lady of their ideals a perfect compliment. Though I know you never told us precisely what fruit attracted the curious hands of our first parents, tradition has complimented you and the apple, which delights our eye and our palate, by making it the forbidden fruit.

Yet roses are not for me; so they are on the altar of Our Lady, and I hope my dear Lord is pleased with them there.

The little hyacinth, however, remains there on my table. Again a kind friend brought it in and told me that it would bloom if each day I watered it. Even my very non-green thumb apparently could not upset the swift progress of this hyacinth. The slim green blade has leaped magically from the little pot. It has spread into half a dozen fingers, out of the palm of which grows the stalk topped with beautiful blooms. They are a silent cluster of Easter bells, ringing out a lovely perfume. Though the weather is still chill and grey outside, they bring spring into my room. It should not be too difficult to dream of the Resurrection when out of the moss-covered earth in the tomb-like pot comes this gracious awakening of life.

I find it inspiring, dear Lord, to be living and praying in the room which witnesses one of your miracles, the blooming of a hyacinth. Out of the strangely fertile elements bound in the little clay pot, nature, which you created, is working its alchemy. Black earth is becoming a proud cluster of white and green and golden beauty. The shapeless water is turning into exquisite symmetry the bright, erect stems and the bell-like blossoms. What power did you give to nature which, under our eyes, so uninterruptedly performs this wonder? Children grow pop-eyed at the magician whose trick consists in making a plant appear out of a cardboard box. I am afraid that I am a little pop-eyed as I watch my watered soil blooming in the swift glory of a springtime flower.

I find it humbling, too, dear Lord. Is this a symbol of my contribution to earth's development? I keep finding myself thinking of the flower as "my hyacinth." When a sweet nun came in, I asked her how she liked "my flower" and told her with some pride how I had been watering it faithfully "until, as you see, it is blossoming into a perfect cluster of beauty." Funny, isn't it, that I should brag when my total contribution has been to bring water from the bathroom tap and pour it on the base of the flower. When all I did was stand aside and watch your wonder develop. My flower, indeed!

You are very wonderful, dear Lord.

Across the street there is much stir and activity. Our lovely Catholic hospital is separated by the width of a side-street from the great hospital complex of an important university medical school. As I sit by the window watching the men at work on a new addition, I find myself contrasting the growth of your hyacinth with the construction of the new building across the way. I'm sure the men at work know their business, yet as I watch them I become aware of the heavy laboriousness of their labor, the loud slowness of their tempo, even though the work yard is powerfully arrayed with the might of muscle and machine. They pause to consult elaborate blueprints and scratch their heads with pencils. They pause while lengths of steel and fresh-cut planks and pieces of pipe are carried here and there. They are fashioning a skeleton of steel which, like the outer bone of one of your primitive sea monsters, will in time disappear.

Great labor at the drawing board, century-old skills, and tools manufactured only last year combine to create this new building. There is much noise of hammers and saws and shouting and wet concrete pouring out of its mixer and planks slapping on cement and steel being dropped into place. In the end, the building will rise, four-square and solid, an ingenious adaptation by your sons of the materials which you stocked up for their use.

Yet I cannot but contrast the sweet hyacinth growing noiselessly and beautifully on my table with the rise of that building across the street. One loves the way you work, quietly, without fuss or confusion, in the magical transubstantiation of earth and water into perfume and texture and beauty of line; while the architect with great labor and sweat and striving and bustle (and usually a share of pride as well) achieves a structure of considerable usefulness but very dubious charm.

Later on, I fancy that in the upper stories of this building laboratories will be opened and chemists will go about their work. If, out of their test tubes, using the materials which you gave them, they succeed in "creating" one blade of grass, the science committee for the Nobel Prize would beg them to accept the honor. If, after years of experimenting, they manage to synthesize the elements of a hyacinth and produce one sickly bloom . . . then headlines will shout, "They have created life!"

You are wonderful, dear Lord, and though we struggle might and main to copy some of your wonder, the best we do is rearrange slightly what you created with extravagant genius.

We water your hyacinth and claim the flower as our own.

We take sand and stone and water from the earth and when we have shaped them into a building, we proudly cry. "I made this and it is mine."

With the casual ease that we can discern in a growing plant, you made the universe. With infinite groaning, mishaps, experiments, and blunders, with noise and outcry, we do our small work.

If we know any pride, surely it should be pride in our Father and our Creator. If we boast, it should be of the world that you have made. If ever we are humble, it ought to be when we stand before the flower we watered, the bricks we laid one on the other, the words we strung together in stuttering ambiguities, our greatest achievements—trifling rearrangements of the patterns of your universe.

You are so great, dear Lord, and I am so small.

Your achievements are the perfect pattern, mine are the pitiful copies.

The angels stand in wondering awe before the results of your creative commands; only I find anything to admire in what I have done.

Yet I am your son; I share your creative urge; I walk in your footsteps; I make because I must, and when I fail, I am miserable and defeated.

Let me add some trifle, if it be only the water at the base of a hyacinth, to your lovely world. But keep me from the stupid pride that cries out that "This is mine!"

Thank you for the hyacinth. Thank you for the impulse that makes the men across the street build strong and well. Thank you for letting me, your son, be a small partner in your work. But let me keep my sense of values. I pause to water your hyacinth and add at the end of my stumbling letter, my only reason for pride: that I am

Your grateful son,

IV

Dear Lord,

In a rather pitying voice, we speak of our fellow men as "entering their second childhood."

It's strange that we have so deep an affection for our first childhood and such smiling pity for our second. Actually, your Son spoke of another second childhood when he insisted that, "Unless we become as little children, we shall not enter the Kingdom of Heaven."

So the very word "child" throws us into confusion.

We are sentimentally attached to our first childhood.

We see in our second childhood a sad collapse of maturity, adulthood running to seed, powers waning, and the dark night setting in.

And all the while, the voice of our Savior orders us to become, willingly and gladly, as little children.

I am your son, dear Lord. Am I also, in the sense that you would approve, your child? I wish I were sure of that. I wish you could smile down upon me with the calm, reassuring affection which a father feels for the toddler at his side.

My mother (another of your major blessings for which I could well spend time right here and now in an act of thanksgiving) used to say that the happiest time of her life was when I was about four. The age of reason was still ahead. But infancy had passed. I could talk. I could companion her on her junkets to the market. I could kneel beside her, however unintelligently, at church. Her greatest joy was when I held tight to her hand and trotted along at her side. Her heart was moved by the implicit confidence with which I clung to her fingers. She could look down to see my eyes turned up to her in complete trust. I was very much aware of her importance to me. I

would burst into tears if she was unexpectedly absent, and I feared
the tragedy of her loss. I chattered to her in the monologue of newly
acquired words and spurts and flashes of ideas.

But she had in all this one great joy: I depended upon her, I
somehow had come to know how much I depended upon her, and
I accepted the dependence gladly and gratefully.

I am sure I was happy then. It was in the years before I knew
sin. The world was bursting around me in the glory of first discovery.
Everything was exciting. Nothing had been staled by use or dulled by
that strange faculty we humans have of growing tired of the things
which serve us constantly and best.

My mother was happy because I depended upon her.

And in the glory of your newly discovered world, I was deeply
happy because I depended upon her.

Isn't it strange, dear Lord, that with the years we grow to dislike
the word "dependence"? Independence is a precious thing to the
people of your American nation. We are a cocky rather than a proud
people, aggressive rather than arrogant. We like the money in our
pockets and wallets and checking accounts and stocks and bonds that
makes us independent. We look forward to an independent old age.
"He's an independent soul," we say in what we regard as a compliment. "Let me be independent," we cry to a paternal government
that seems to be coddling us.

Yet when we were dependent, we were deeply happy.

Well, Lord, this is meant to be a happy letter. Old as I am, and
verging on or merging into my second childhood, I should like to
reimagine for myself the dependence which once made my mother
and myself so happy. I am afraid that I have often been proud of my
independence. I have gloried, not like your son Paul in my weakness,
but in my confident strength. I have not liked to cling. I have been
pleased when I could look down upon "dependents," as I mentally

termed them, who hung tightly to my hands or who trusted my advice.

Because I was a religious, you wanted me to know the humiliating dependence of obedience. I dodged that with too much success. That was part of the return to childhood which Christ commended and I avoided.

Now voluntarily, I take my place among your children. This morning I am less your son than your very little, stumbling, dependent child. For such I always am, and such, apparently, you prefer me to be. I reach up to take the strong hand of my Father. I walk not alone in my confidence but by your side in voluntary dependence. I would not be strong today but weak, not sure of myself but very sure of you, not leading the way but walking with an effort to match your stride, not caring where I go so long as you take me there.

It is good to hold your hand, to look up and almost see your deep, paternal eyes resting upon me. It is good to say, "Today I shall make no decisions for myself or for others; but I shall put everything completely in his hands." If I stumble, he will not let me fall. If I chatter, he will listen and make sense of my jargon. When I am tired, I will lean a little more heavily and his strength will carry me along.

Perhaps it seems like a beautiful fantasy.

It may be the dreamy imaginings of age.

Except, dear Lord, for the wonderful fact that it is the truth.

Always I am, all of us are, your little children. Always you are the Father who is never happier (though why, I am not altogether sure) than when we cling to you, trot along beside you, look up at you in utter confidence, and speak to you with our new-learned words.

We may play at independence; we remain totally dependent. We may act self-assured; we are sure of very little. We may strut, but usually as prelude to our stumble.

Yet what, on the other hand, could be more reassuring than this very dependence? I am dependent, but upon whom? Upon the all-powerful God that you are. Upon the all-loving Father that you are. Upon the provident Benefactor that you are. I am dependent not upon weakness or caprice, but upon unchangeable goodness. I hold to the creative hand of my God, the unchanging love of my Lord, the inexhaustible generosity of my King, the untiring patience of my Father.

It is good for me to think of my dependence upon you. It is good, humiliating, and infinitely reassuring.

I look through my bright window into the crisp, sun-warmed winter's day. Dependent? Dear Lord, what if this morning you had forbidden the sun to rise? What panic would now fill the streets! What terror would drive us in aimless whirling circles of wild surmise and consultation!

Unless I pause to remember it, I do not realize that I have been sitting here breathing in and out the wonderful thing which is the air you created. At the end of the hospital corridor is a balanced fish bowl. In it serenely swim half a dozen goldfish, lazily circling in and out of their underwater pagoda, ruffling slightly the weeds that grow in vivid green in their domain. They do not know what I know; that someone who cared for them protectively had balanced the weeds so that the water would be constantly fresh, the oxygen supply adequate, so that they could swim about in peace and confidence, their gills opening and closing as nature requires.

I am not comparing myself, dear Lord, to a goldfish. And yet, I am. For I move in the vast goldfish bowl which is your atmosphere. Not so long ago, I read for the first time a study of earth's atmosphere, and I bowed my head before yet another of your wonders. I had never known how it worked, this air around us. And now, after reading the article, I know only vaguely—about the gases that rise from the vegetation of the seas, the plants that absorb these gases and transform them into atmosphere, the trees that fountain out the water necessary to make the air easy on my lungs, the waiting chemistry of the plants that picks up the foul air I exhale and turns it back into wholesome atmosphere. I do not understand it, dear Lord; I just marvel at my complete dependence upon you, at my childish acceptance of your wonders without surprise or gratitude.

I recall how, when I was studying my philosophy (and again my thanks for that privilege, one of your great gifts), a professor compared life to a chain. Or was this something you taught me in a moment of prayer rather than of study? I saw myself as the last link in the chain of life, not the last but the latest. I saw myself hanging from my immediate ancestors who hung in turn from the long line of the human race. I recall that I puzzled at the time whether you made the world directly, each species according to its kind, or created it by the greater wonder of evolution. In any case, I, this little link at the end of timeless history, swung from the links above, and up, up until the chain vanished from recorded history into the years before men wrote down their records. And then I saw the chain swinging in vast oceans of time, those geologic ages about which we talk with such casual ease, as people are always sure of things they have not seen and places they have not been. Up and up the chain swung in vanishing lines of faint perspective. But it did not disappear. It could not suddenly end in empty space. For if it did, it would, like a chain unattached to a hook in the roof, come clattering down in clanky confusion. No, though I could not see the hand that held it, I knew the hand was there, and I knew the hand was yours. Quite literally, dear Lord, I depended. I hung like the final link in an incredible chain held by a sustaining hand. Your hands have bent the first link into its sure pattern. The other links came in their right order, however you willed them to come; until finally there was the little minor link, myself.

But far, far up there in infinite space was your strong, sure, gentle hand sustaining the chain, sustaining me.

I depend upon you.

. . . for the eyes which miraculously camera the lovely world you created for my service and delight . . .

. . . for my mind and the truth that must fill it . . .

. . . for my body and the food and light and water and air that keep it going . . .

. . . for friendship and love and books and music, for the service of animals and the mercy of men and the gentleness of women . . .

. . . for health, your gift, and sickness, often your greater gift, for laughter and the sense of humor, for the power to run and the instinct to create, for the birth of children, and the release from old age of gentle death.

I depend upon you, dear Lord, and the thought should make me deeply humble and wonderfully glad.

The proudest among us cannot shake off that dependence. Yet it irritates the proud. They are angry that they must take time for food or cannot live in the rarefied atmosphere of Mount Everest. They fight their dependence upon sweet sleep and are annoyed that they must ask the assistance of their fellow men.

Most of all they resent their dependence upon you.

They are like sulky children (how often I have been!) who suddenly jerk their fingers out of the hand of their father and cry, "Let me walk alone." They slap down the gentle hand that reaches out to steady and guide them.

Wasn't it Kipling who wrote familiar lines that run something like this:

> For down to Gehenna or up to the Throne
> He travels the fastest who travels alone.

I wonder how true that is? Science has moved with amazing speed since individual inventors working in their garrets or cellars gave place to the teams of scientists working together. The solitary rower in a fishing craft gets out of the way of the magnificent united effort which is the ocean liner and its trained crew. If Kipling's saying is true, would you have instituted the partnership of marriage? Would you have asked your religious to unite in communities, working together for your glory and the happiness of mankind?

Probably only half of that is really true. Down to Gehenna, yes, I guess the child travelling alone may travel swiftly indeed. He's the single skier flying down a precipitous mountain side—to the unseen rocks below. He is the solitary parachutist dropping from a plane into the jungle. He is the carnival diver plunging from his lofty perch into the tank of water topped by spectacular flames.

It is easy to go to Hell alone. Indeed, dear Lord, if one is without your sustaining hand and wise direction, how can a man escape the easy downgrade to ruin?

But up to the Throne? Ah, dear Lord, how badly I need you! How completely I depend upon you!

Without you, I do not know the way; I have not got the strength; I will be lost; I will stumble and fall to my ruin.

So like the little child I am, I reach up, dear Lord, for your hand. I feel the warmth and reassurance of your fingers. I begin to talk to you and your gentle eyes turn down to regard me with flattering attention. My wearying steps become eager strides. If I stumble, I laugh gaily and hang more tightly to your arm. If the way is dark, I know confidence in my guide. And somehow just ahead I am sure that there is the dawning of a sunrise brighter than any of earth, and the breath of perfume from a glorious garden, and the faint sound of music lovelier than any I have ever heard.

I am happy, dear Lord, for I walk depending upon you.

Does it make you, as it made my mother, a little happy, too, that I cling so trustingly to your hand?

Your devoted son,

V

Dear Lord,

This letter is begun with considerable hesitation.

It may have an arrogant sound. It may even seem a positive impertinence. It was a joyful thing to be able to write to you, as I did recently, "I depend upon you, dear Lord, and I joyfully accept that humbling and exalting fact." But I am not sure how it sounds when I write, as now I do, "And for some strange reason, Lord, you depend upon me."

That is a thought which has been disturbing me recently.

When I write, "I depend upon you," the whole universe seems in right order; the little hangs from the big; the weak rests upon the strong; the stupid turns toward the wise; the creature takes his place below the creator.

But when I write, "And you, Lord, depend upon me . . . ," I find myself gulping, glowing with an unmistakable blush, ashamed of apparent arrogance, and not quite sure that I am expressing the startling truth correctly.

Yet I can see no other explanation for the universe and no other plan in life. Up to the coming of man, everything is precision and order. The stars move with such exactitude that we set our watches by the swing of distant planets through space. The laws of nature hold with such inflexible rigor that scientists can predict without doubt what evening star will be shining in June of the year 2935. What happens in a test-tube today will happen a thousand years from now. And each confident dawn we rise, put our feet out of bed, and have no fear that the law of gravity might have been repealed during the night.

The instinct of the animals is a predictable thing. Each year, the swallows will return to Capistrano to the slight bewilderment of the ornithologist, the delight of the tourist, and the inspiration of the song writer.

The swallows nest in Radio City the way they did in the newly built pyramids. The life cycle of an amoeba has not changed in a hundred million years. And the wheat that grew under the provident eye of Joseph, governor of Egypt, yielded itself in nourishing food then as it does when harvested on the plains of Kansas.

Then into the world appears of a sudden the strange, mysterious, capricious, largely unpredictable creature who is man. I am an amazing creature, dear Lord, and I say that in bewilderment, not in pride. I have a thousand laws in my nature by which I breathe and grow and feel and walk and breed and die. And I have a lawlessness that can see the law and trample on it, recognize my own greatest good and reject it, look on the truth and prefer the lie, know my happiness and choose my sorrow, read the signposts along the road to success and tear them down as I turn to the dark, forbidding, repellent path to failure.

And as I do these strangely lawless things in your lawful world, as I run amok to the amazement of your well-ordered creatures, apparently you stand aside as if you could not stop me.

I am the one element of disorder in history.

I am the only creature constantly upsetting the applecart.

I am the outlaw in the civilization you created.

I am the rebel in the midst of universal obedience.

It is all very terrible and frightening . . . and inspiring and challenging. It is terrible that I can be a high explosive blowing up the order and happiness around me. It frightens me that I can wreck what with beautiful planning you created. But I am inspired with the truth that while you made the plants and the planets, fire and foxes, larks and lions, rainbows and reindeer, electrons and elephants completely subject to your law, you made me free. It is a challenge to realize how far you have trusted me.

From what you have told me, dear Lord, it seems you must have experimented twice with freedom. Once you made your angels free, and some of them used their free will in cataclysmic rebellion. They invented the explosive thing called sin. They rocked the heavens and blew open the jagged, stinking shell hole of Hell. One blast of their rebel cry, and the angelic faces were twisted into the demoniac masks they will forever wear.

Perhaps, dear Lord, we become so preoccupied with the hideous creatures who are fallen angels, the devils, that we forget the multitudes who used their freedom to remain faithful, your angels. I can never understand why we find the sinner more fascinating than the saint. We are more absorbed in the story of murder than in the story of martyrdom. The pure seem pallid beside the lurid coloring of the lustful. And devils have in art been terrifyingly alive creatures while angels have tended to freeze into calm, stony lifelessness.

At any rate, I cannot let myself forget, dear Lord, that your first gift of freedom divided the world of that eternal day into the Hosts of Heaven and the Hordes of Hell, the glorious angels who flash their beauty across our Christmas and Easter sky, and the devils who hunched upon pagan altars, disguised themselves in the bodies of snakes, and copied the ugliest features of wild beasts and madmen.

That same freedom was your gift to me. And with it, you constituted the strangest possible relationship between us: you made yourself dependent upon me.

I shall always be completely dependent upon you for food and air and light for mind and eye. Physically I can never be even slightly independent of you. Yet you permitted—no, you *willed*—a dependence upon me to which I can never grow completely accustomed. Up to a point you would make the world perfect; at that point you would turn it over to my free management. Your word of creation would bring into perfect order the universe in which I live; but your word to me was spoken in an entirely different tone: "My

son, I am trusting you from this point on. Will you do well for me
and by my world?"

At that moment, your strange dependence upon me begins.

You give me all the elements which will make my life a success;
I am free to shuffle these elements in such a fashion that they spell
out failure.

Into the orbit of my influence, you send the people who are
your sons and daughters. For them you have done all that is necessary
for their happiness. Yet I am able to ruin their happiness, steal from
them, trick and fool them, lay lustful or murderous hands upon their
bodies or their souls, betray them with false words, bad example,
wrong directions, evil in a million attractive or repellent forms.

The world around us is as ordered as the atom in a chunk of
uranium. I may wrench it from its calm course to destroy a civilization. I can take your gift of speech and with it make fair words
mask foul intentions. My hands, meant to build, can pull down into
shattering ruins. My power of creation can become the power of
perversion. I can foment a rebellion against you and your sons and
daughters, forcing your creatures to serve me, and using the powers
with which you filled the earth to wreck the earth and awaken the
howls and tears of earth-dwellers.

Sometimes it must almost seem that the history of mankind
is a long record of betrayals. One reads the history of religions, and
along the calm current of your true religion are the thousand ugly,
twisting canals of the false. For one altar lifted in calm serenity to
bear gifts to you, a thousand altars have carried gifts to imposters. For
one clear voice singing out your truth, great choruses have chanted
their discord.

The happy country, they say, has no history.

If that is true, how few happy countries there must have
been! For the volumes of wars and conquests, of murdered kings
and weeping queens, of oppressed peoples and nameless slaves, of

misleading leaders and men of power whom power corrupted, of prophets caught by their own false prophecies, of tyrants deified because they were in such ungodly fashion cruel, of empires striding proudly to glory and decaying into oblivion—these volumes fill the libraries of the world.

Along with great heroism, greater selfishness. Cancelling out generosity, a larger greed. Men of truth battling against the thousands who loved the convenient small lie and invented the staggering Big Lie. Men who loved their fellow men undone by those who knew only lust. City walls raised to protect stolen goods, retain captured slaves, drive away the beggars at the gate, and bar you, dear Lord, entrance.

Yet you stand aside, dependent upon your children.

You made us free, and you will not destroy our freedom even when our freedom destroys your world.

You turned the world over to our management, and though our management may drive it into bankruptcy, you will not go back on your part of the bargain.

You could have created us in the perfectly ordered world of the ant or the bee. Winter and summer we would have slaved in our little civilizations, unmarked by rebellions, undisturbed by sin. Instead you let us build Egypt and Assyria, Rome and Venice, and the British Empire. We might, like blind moles, have endlessly fertilized your earth as we burrowed in the dark avenues underground. You let us build our military roads and send our caravans of commerce across the world and gather our fleets and march our armies.

Our dances might have been the beautiful dances of the stars. They could have been as innocent as daffodils dancing in an April wind, or the gracious minuet of golden wheat. We might dance before the Ark, the Tabernacle, or the monstrance. But we have danced instead before a brazen serpent, a golden calf, in Saturnalia, or Bacchanalia, or strip-tease.

I can understand a great many things in your wonderful world, dear Lord. Your trust in your sons and daughters is more than I can comprehend. Surely you knew how often we would fail you. Certainly you were aware that you were putting great powers in untrustworthy hands. You knew us far better than the greatest historian can know us from a study of our endless delinquencies. Yet you put yourself into our power. You turned so large a section of your world over to us.

Your confidence never wavered. Your trust was never withdrawn. You left yourself dependent upon us . . . as you are now dependent upon me.

It's quite simple for me to describe your dependence on human beings against an historical background. So easy to blame the dead who failed you and the tyrants and villains who betrayed your trust.

What bothers me are my own betrayals. What must not happen again is my failure of responsibility. Mine has been a small world, yet I have managed to mess it up tragically. You gave me a limited talent, but enough to have used it for great glory to you and real happiness to others. Maybe it's better if I don't go into that right now. It will make the mystery of your dependence seem more mysterious still. In the dimness of my constant failures, I am simply baffled by the fact that you still permit yourself to depend upon me.

But you do, dear Lord; you do.

You give me all the graces necessary to be a saint. But you will not force sainthood on me. Whether or not I am a saint depends upon my use of your gifts.

You give me the associates and friends who are in the orbit of my small universe. I had almost rather not pause to realize how much their goodness, their happiness, their peace, their right direction, their life here and their destiny hereafter, may depend upon me. Surely I should be a fool to pretend that I am the sun or stars or moon to anyone; yet even the wild meteor or the minor satellite has its effect upon the universe . . . and so have I upon mine.

Often in retreats to others I have said what must be one of the great platitudes: "God has given you a place in his plan. If you fulfill it, he will be pleased and his plan will be perfected. If you fail him, there is nothing that even God can do about it." Then, you remember, at great length I have talked of how you depend upon each of us and all of us, the greatest and the smallest.

It was easy to say that to others because it is transparently true. Now I say it to myself, and I am afraid.

My God, you depend upon me.

What happens in my soul is not the result of miracles of grace but of grace which I may use or neglect as I wish. You depend on me.

What happens in my association with others is no matter of great inspirations or the separation of the waters of the Red Sea. It is just the conjunction of my opportunities to do good, which you graciously send me, and my acceptance of those opportunities, which is entirely up to me.

If I work, the work is done. If I loaf, the work stands still. If I pray, the effects of prayer follow. If I do not pray, I leave behind me a spiritual vacuum. If I speak the right words—not the wise words but the wholesome words, not the clever words but the sincere ones—truth knows a fresh gleam in a confused age. If I speak the wrong ones . . . the foolish, the vain, the lying, the soiled . . . dear Lord, forgive them even if you cannot undo their harm.

When I was a child, you allowed me to come to know the popular novel of the period, *Little Lord Fauntleroy*. Of the story which remains rather vague to me, there stands out one scene: young Lord Fauntleroy coming down the stairs accompanied by his distinguished old grandfather, a Duke, if I recall correctly. And as they come to the landing the small boy in all confidence says to his grandfather, "Lean on me, Grandfather!" And without a smile or a hesitation, the fine old gentleman accepts the help.

I have a vivid image of that scene, the small boy, the tall vigorous old man, the hand which had known many a great achievement, resting firmly on the shoulder of his young companion, the youngster proudly serving as a prop for his grandsire.

Maybe the Duke needed the help. Maybe he accepted some that helped him not at all. What does it matter? A small boy wanted to be of help. A youngster was deeply proud that his much admired grandfather placed his hand trustingly on his shoulder. Age became briefly dependent on youth. Experience leaned on inexperience.

Is it farfetched that I see a connection, dear Lord? What possible need could you have for my shoulder? Why should you lean on me? Yet you do. You do just that. I am grateful. It is a challenge and a trust, an inspiration and a call to character. If you are willing to depend upon me, weak, stupid, clumsy, bad as I am, I am eager not to fail you.

Lean on me, dear Lord. At least pretend to find me a help. And your sweet pretense may make me worthy of your very real trust.

Your grateful son,

Daniel

VI

Dear Lord,

Almost more than anything else I have dreaded being a bore.

That's my pride, isn't it! That's just because I know how people despise a bore, how writers have pilloried them, and how even their friends and relatives run from them.

Well, I have been looking back over the sins of a year . . . a horrifying and grim experience . . . and I have decided that I am the world's prize bore. The sins of the year have been numerous as the sands of the sea. And like the sands they are gritty, and oh, so dreadfully the same.

Often, dear Lord, as I have sat in your confessional dispensing your mercies to penitent daughters and prodigal sons, I have felt myself sighing, "Oh, what a bore!" Not that it wasn't a joy and a privilege to be able to lift my hand in absolution over sin-sick souls. I knew myself the happiness that follows the priestly, "Go in peace," a form of farewell that your Son, Jesus, taught us. But the sins themselves . . .

So tiresome.

So repetitious.

So utterly without imagination.

Perhaps my course of moral theology slightly misled me. You recall that I had a brilliant and oh, so gentle and humanly understanding a teacher in Father O'Boyle. He had a charming flow of speech. He touched human failings with a tender hand, and, preparing us for the labors of our physicianly office, he was far less concerned with pointing out the ugliness and horror of sin than in indicating what made sinners sick, and how the symptoms of bad habits could be forestalled, and what to do when the dead soul was

39

placed at your feet or the sick whisper-confessed that hope was gone and spiritual health seemed impossible to hold.

There was a pity in his voice that no one could miss. He was never the thundering judge but always the devoted doctor. He was not preparing us for the confessional as for a law court, but as for the sick room of a crowded hospital, where death must be held back and health restored, and, if humanly possible, relapses prevented.

Yet the thickness of the volume we studied I'm afraid misled us. It listed so many kinds and categories of sins. It seemed to record so many ways in which people could offend you. It ran from big and spectacular sins down to small, termite vices. It presented the basic offenses and the strange, discordant obbligatos which sinners had written around them.

I studied hard, preparing myself to be a good physician of souls.

Then with the years, I came to know the painful monotony of sinners. Almost never did a sinner show (forgive me for putting it this way) one slightest glimmer of originality. There was no such thing as a fresh vice, just the tiresome repetition of old ones.

I recall when I read a biography of poor Oscar Wilde (whom in the end you mercifully snatched from ruin on his death bed) I had a sort of oblique hope. Here was a man who would twist a beautiful old truth in order to create a shining new lie. Yet the sin for which he suffered, a sin which he obviously thought was singularly pioneering and in his age novel and startling, was the sin of the ancient Greeks, the dreadfully tiresome perversion for which you rained fire and brimstone upon the cities of the plain.

In the dull litany of confessions, one slightly different sin would stand out with startling hue, a bright scarlet, a blinding green. But seldom was I jolted by any flash of freshness in sinning. The long, plodding parade of recurrent weaknesses and human faults and the common sins of an age and a class and even a time of year.

From your throne above, dear Lord, do you see anything more tiresome, as surely you see nothing more dreadful, than the monotony of our sins?

Of course I've heard it said a thousand times that the one thing man really contributed to creation is his sin. That was the only thing you did not make. Everything but sin and vice and rebellion, the lust of the body and the pride of the mind and the greed of the hands and the lies of the tongue was yours. Sin was our one notable contribution to the universe.

If that be true, then perhaps that explains its magnificent monotony. You never made two oak leaves the same. No sand crystals are identical. No two oysters or clams or jellyfish are exactly alike. In a pansy bed, each little face is distinctive. The ears of corn are individual. And every human face since Adam's has known that mark of the great artist—freshness, clear differences of line and expression, a unique identity.

But when man comes to the thing he does most successfully and constantly—sin—what a tiresome, monotonous job he turns out. He becomes almost like a machine, stamping out innumerable gadgets each undistinguishable from the other.

It is no wonder that sin and vice challenge the ingenuity of the writer. You do not need to deck out virtue and goodness in anything but its simple grace. It is beautiful in itself. Virtue is infinitely varied. Goodness may be a copy of any of the infinite perfections the saint discovers in you. But sin . . . ah, there is dread and dull stuff, and the writer sets himself the task of making it seem fascinating, amusing, imaginative, exciting, ingenious . . . which it simply never is.

I have heard it said that there are not more than a dozen basic dirty stories in the world. Liars fall into a pattern of lying, as painters might adopt a pattern of painting. Police come to know the work of thieves by the constant repetition of a single method. And what is conceivably more tiresome than the endless gossip of the uncharitable?

So, dear Lord, I look back upon my life knowing that I am a bore.

There may have been some freshness in a sermon or two I gave; there was none in my sinning.

I may have written an occasional line that had some originality. In my sins, I copied a pattern old as the dreadful first years that followed Eden.

Thanks to the inspiration of your grace, I may have had flashes of prayer that had about them the slight flavor of poetry. My words of unkindness and impatience were as old as the first jealous heart and shrewish mouth.

Wouldn't you think I'd learn, dear Lord, how tiresome sin is? Wouldn't you think that sometime or other I'd master the obvious: that the consequences of sin are the most tiresome of human experience? Why do I always think that this sin will be different and that this time it will not be followed with disillusionment, a dark brown taste, a pain in the head and an emptiness in the heart, embarrassment and the humiliating conviction of failure?

I suppose sin is so dreadfully boresome because it is a negative. After a strong affirmation, anything will or may happen. "Will you build here?" a man is asked. "Yes," he answers firmly, and on the bare plot of land any of a thousand things may rise. "Will you build here?" a man is asked. "No," he answers flatly, and from nothing, nothing follows.

I suppose sin is so pointless and repetitious because it is so destructive. There are a hundred ways to build. You knock down the loveliest temple and the most miserable hut with the same iron ball.

I am sorry that where sin is concerned, I am such a bore, dear Lord. My confessions—what a stereotyped performance they represent. I could almost run off a mimeographed sheet and present it to my patient confessor. The gamut of my sinning is so totally without flare or imagination. If the booklets I wrote all treated the same subject in the same words, I should be ashamed to say they were mine. The sins I repeat endlessly without any realization that I am such a tiresome lout!

Was there something divinely deliberate that limited our power of sinning to such a small mouthful of words and such feeble sweeps of our fists, such appetites common to the wisest and the most vulgar, the same cruelties that reduce us all to beasts? Sometimes I think that we resemble the beasts only when we sin. They are ingenious in the lairs they build, the ways they hunt their food, the vast variety of their instincts. They gulp with a common greed; they lust with a swift, almost reckless avidity; they claw in almost involuntary strokes; they take life with a singular lack of planning. In our sins, we are like the beasts. The less like the beasts we are in our sinning, the less brutal or beastly or cruel or insensate, heedless of consequences, the braver, more thoughtful, kinder, the higher our virtue, the fuller is our humanity.

Dear Lord, forgive me for the sins which year after year I repeat routinely.

Dear Lord, forgive me for the thousand promises, all alike in their wording, and all unkept in a brief lapse of time.

Dear Lord, forgive me for the same annoyances I cause to others, the same, dull bad example which sets back your work.

I am sorry for the tiresome sound of repeated tears and wailing, for the recurrent pattern of patchwork following wars, and rubble heaps where once stood peaceful homes and prosperous cities.

I am ashamed to be of the race of sinners, whose sins are always the same, whose remorse and disillusionment are always the same old story.

I am ashamed that I, who should so like to be a model of originality, a creator of the new and fresh, a disdainer of the stale cliché should in my sins, my personal vices, my feeble words of sorrow, my imperfect purpose of amendment, my swift return to habits with which I am deeply wearied, should be in your eyes . . . and now my own . . . a tiresome bore.

Your deeply apologetic son,

Daniel

VII

Dear Lord,

If I should fail, I'm afraid I have no excuse.

Perhaps it may not be smart to put myself on record this way. One should keep an excuse within easy reach, in the event of failure. But this morning, in all honesty, I look in vain for such an excuse. And that rather frightens me.

Except of course for the fact that you have no intention of letting me fail. Your power and your grace are at my disposal to head off the possibility of failure. You do not want it; you will do all I allow you to prevent it; you know with infinite clarity the consequences to me of failure. It is not, certainly, in your plan.

Yet it is important for me to remember that I can fail. I shall be safe, as a wise old priest used to say, fifteen minutes after I am dead. I shall be confirmed in success only when your judgment has been rendered in my personal judgment, with the records all before your eyes, and some expert accountant in the person, I suppose, of a particularly wise and impartial seraph, rendering the final audit.

I am writing a little frivolously about it right now because frankly I am feeling far from frivolous. If there were as many mistakes in the books of any cashier as there are in mine, he would spend a long time thinking that over in Leavenworth or Atlanta, our earthly hells for the defaulters. I am frightened when I think back over my life. Things are far from in order for the arrival of that bank examiner, death. Never in my life have I done anything that was not marred by fault, mistake, selfishness, or evil. Never have I done a perfect work. And my sins . . .

Your prophet centuries ago begged you to forgive him the forgotten sins of his youth. Forgetfulness is not the same thing as repentance. That we forget doesn't mean that you necessarily forgive.

So without the wastefulness and luxury of scruples, I am apologizing now for sins which I have forgotten. May I say in a blanket apology that if ever I offended you, failed in my duty, spoiled your work or your plans and your hopes, I am deeply sorry.

The sins of my youth were sins of impulse or weakness or juvenile passion. The sins that mark the years are of a different and darker tinge. Whether they in themselves seem greater or less, they were committed in maturity, with a clear mind, with knowledge and forethought, with some perception of their evil, and much experience of the ugly consequences of sin.

I have failed you over and over again, and I wish I could say, "Ah, but I have an excuse." Believe me, I am not flattering myself with superhuman strength when I know I am without extenuation; I am simply aware of the abundance of your grace and strength poured into my soul. Where I failed it was with a kind of deliberate rejection of your outstretched hand. I struck it down rather than let it hold me firmly erect. When my soul seemed weak, it was because I would not let your grace nourish it. My failures were a kind of deliberately planned collapse. I was not tricked or deceived or seized with a sudden spiritual vertigo. I deliberately risked walking along the edge.

All this is what worries me today, and I intend that it shall be allowed to worry me. I shall not turn my eyes to convenient weaknesses of character which you know and I know. Let others who may have partnered my lapse go scot free today. I will not copy my first father's lame excuse of laying the blame on another's head. Truth demands that I take full blame. And now I do.

It is wiser that I do it now than belatedly when I face your judgment seat. And even that embarrassing prospect is new reason for gratitude. For the memory of my own sinning brings back the clear memory of your goodness. My weakness serves to underline your offer of strength. My failure was clearly preceded by the rejection of your proffered help. Because you were so good, my failures stand out in clear relief.

That is why I know I have no excuse.

The General Judgment will be, I'm sure, a time of great surprises for everyone, dear Lord, but you. We have a way, we humans, of lumping together all men and women, as if all had the same natural gifts and supernatural endowments. We talk of heredity and environment in the science classroom, but pay little attention to them in measuring the conduct of those who harm us or annoy us. We expect good manners of those who come from the slums, and honesty from the nomad brought up to regard theft as an honorable profession. We turn in disgust from the fallen woman who slipped into her sins when she was still a child. We are repelled by the cruelty of men who as children knew little else around them. We resent the crimes of children who were raised in the sin-created slums of our cities.

By all that I shall have a tough time of it.

To whom much has been given, from his much is expected. And you have given me so much that I have no excuse.

Would you mind, dear Lord, if, just for my own sake, I were to imagine the scene of the Judgment and my failure? You have warned me repeatedly that it is possible for me to fail. I have not overlooked the fact that Solomon, wisest of all men, failed; and Judas, who came to your Son in the youthful outpouring of his native generosity; and that the history of the failures of the Church has been the collapse of bishops and priests who could attack the truth so brilliantly because they had been trained by study and by grace to know it and love and defend it. I cannot forget that St. Paul prayed that while he preached to others he might not himself become a castaway. I cannot escape the fact that my flesh will ever lust against my spirit.

I recall that your Son warned us to pray always, that he seemed to brood over his disciples when, after three years in their companionship, he knew that they would run from the first threatening sword.

I can fail, and if I fail, I shall have no excuse.

Let me imagine myself standing in your presence. It is hard, dear Lord, to imagine you unsmiling. This beautiful day on which I look out is like your habitually gracious smile. Now there is a frown veiling your glory . . . your brow is thundered over with anger . . .

"Is this yours?" you ask, as the Recording Angel presents you the balance sheet of my life. Your voice is low and rumbling with regret, disappointment, and just anger.

How wonderful if by some miracle I could deny it. "Of course not, Lord. You know that I'd not be such a fool as to end life with my record in red ink."

No chance of denying the fact; it is mine and you know it and I know it . . . and for a moment it seems as if the whole universe knew it and turned away in disgust at the record of my bankruptcy.

"It is mine, Lord," you hear me answer—the answer wrenched reluctantly from my frightened lips. At that moment, I would give all the joys and satisfactions I had ever known if I could just say, "My Lord." But you are not mine any longer. I cannot claim you.

Your eyes glance at the record. Though you are wordless, I can follow you as you read through your gifts to me—the parents you selected, the nation that was to be mine, the natural abilities with which you endowed me, baptism before I knew consciousness, health, protection . . . and on and on. You seem to read slowly, less to humiliate me than to reassure yourself. You seem to be looking for something you missed, some gift you might have given and withheld, some grace that you might divinely have forgotten. But your side of the ledger is magnificent.

I cringe as your eyes move to my side. At that moment I shall, I'm sure, need no record to remind me of what I did badly, did in evil, failed to do in good. I shall need no nudge from my Guardian

Angel. No taunting devil will need to shake a triumphant finger as he cries, "On such and such a day in such and such a place . . ." Why call for witnesses against me, when the terror I know is the most convincing evidence that could be produced?

The mark of baptism on my soul seems to shine with insistent light. But the mark of confirmation brands me for what I am, a treasonous soldier of the King, a rebel from the ranks, a trafficker with our enemies.

Yet one mark shines out in vivid brilliance.

"What mark is that upon your spirit?" you ask, as if reluctant to believe what you have seen.

Now I should love to be able to deny it, to rub it out with my palm, to tear it from my soul and bury it out of sight. Instead, I answer, "It is the mark of my priesthood."

Even as I say that, I seem to hear a sigh from the whole assembled court of Heaven. Behind me, waiting to be judged, are other souls . . . Moslems from South Arabia, costermongers for the slums of London, men who had left school in third grade, inmates of asylums, pariahs who had begged with cups between their knees on the banks of the Ganges. They regard me with amazement that now I should be lower in the eyes of saints and angels than they. Can it be that I looked down condescendingly on these people in life? Can it be that now they pity me?

You speak once more, as if you hoped there might be some mistake, something that had been overlooked.

"You have, I hope, some excuse, some extenuating circumstances for your failure?"

Are those my lips that give or groan the terrible answer? And was any single word more dreadful, more devastating, more completely condemnatory than the one I speak?

"None, Lord!"

Let's close it there, Lord. I would prefer not to imagine you as you lift your hand to pronounce sentence. I should rather not feel the shudder that runs through the court.

Let's close this letter before I hear the word "Depart!" For that I must never hear. That I must never know. Your final anger must never sear me. I cannot bear the thought of your surrendering my soul to the devil to be his forever.

I have no excuse, Lord, if I fail. Let me never know failure.

Your penitent son,

Daniel

VIII

Dear Lord,

Children can make things ridiculously simple, can't they? (How does it happen, then, that your children make things so complicated for themselves and others? But that's another matter entirely.) When I was very young, we children had reduced the word "vocation" to one very clear fact: the call to be a priest or a nun. Later, under your wonderful Christian Brothers, I enlarged it to include brothers, but as a child even they had not entered my picture.

"Do you think you have a vocation?" We asked ourselves that in our simple little retreats, and tried to imagine ourselves wearing a Roman collar and—incredible glory—saying Mass. And the girls tried to look prim as they mentally decked themselves out in a nun's habit and prefixed "Sister Mary" to their Christian names.

In a vague kind of way we knew that the word—and the fact—implied a calling. Only later we learned that "vocation" and "calling" were synonyms. People, we were convinced, might stumble into other walks of life; they were officially "called" only to the altar and to the cloister.

I can hardly recall a time when I had not heard talk of "the voice of God." For a generation that paid astonishingly little attention to what you said, dear Lord, we still must have talked considerably about your voice.

The voice of God, I was told at an early age, is really the voice of God deep down in my soul. When I told my first lie and that voice spoke to me, I was amazed how loud and terrifying your voice could be.

The Scriptures were the voice of God recorded in imperishable pages. No wonder there was such incomparable eloquence in the words that rolled from the pulpit over my youthful head! In the brogued voice of a man, your words were music and thunder.

We came to wait, as time went on, for the moment when "vocation" would call us . . . or your voice would remain silent. Some lucky ones among us might hear you say, "Come, follow me!" For the rest, life would be lived in the realization that you had not called us. We were not among the many who were called or the few who were chosen.

It took me a long time to understand the simple truth that you call to us every moment of our lives. I was much older before I began to hear your voice all around me. You had placed me in this lovely world and left it to my direction and management, but you did not become a silent partner. You were not voiceless when all the other forces around me were making noise. You called to me and spoke to me and whispered to me and if I listened, life could be lived under the direct guidance of your voice.

Once not so long ago, I wrote complaining a little that when I spoke to you in prayer, I could not hear your answering voice. Now I find myself wondering why you need speak just in answer to prayer when your voice is, if I am giving half-attention, the most constant sound in my life.

I am of course deeply flattered, dear Lord, that when I asked myself in young maturity the childish question, "Have I a vocation?" the answer came with convincing clarity. It was not the young Jesuit scholastic, Mr. Pernin (whose soul long since, I hope and pray, has known the beatific vision) whose voice replied. It was not my own reluctant Yes that seemed forced from my heart, however I might have protested. It was your voice, your call, your invitation, your command. And though I had clapped my hands over my ears and turned to a thousand conflicting sounds to drown out your voice, I could not mistake it and in the end I was for once wise enough not to refuse.

For that vocation I am most grateful.

Yet now as I look back, it seems to me that all life is a series of linked vocations, that your voice calls at every major and minor moment of life.

I shall never forget the revelation which came to me when, under the guidance of my novice master, I knew that all life is a calling. I had never thought how you called me forth from the void of nothingness and gave me a body and a soul, a name and an identity, a place in your scheme of things and the natural powers and the supernatural graces necessary to fulfill your hopes for me. Only Adam had been so called into existence, I once had thought. Your creative "*fiat*" was reserved for the first creation, not for the making of each of your sons and daughters.

I am glad that your voice calls each of us into life. I am glad that while our mothers and fathers unite in the creation of our bodies, your imperial and yet gently paternal voice calls from nothingness our soul. I like to think that you are the first to call each of us by our given name. There is something for me ineffably charming in the belief that it was you who first called me Daniel. May I be permitted a little glow of vanity that mine is an ancient Hebrew name, the tongue which the saints thought might well be spoken in the Courts of Heaven.

The call into life was my first vocation, my first response to the invitation of your voice. In this I had no choice. I bow gratefully to the memory of my parents who accepted their vocation of father and mother and who in the generosity of their hearts shared with me their bodies as you shared with me your spiritual nature.

The second invitation was an even more splendid thing.

Through the ages you had from time to time called favored individuals out of pagandom. You had selected that strange father of all true believers, Abraham, with a voice unique and world-shaking. You had let your voice sound out above music and commerce and the marching of armies when you summoned Moses in his vocation as leader of his people. Indeed the whole Jewish people had the unique vocation and calling which made them different from all other tribes and peoples. You had called them and they had, with whatever reluctance and hesitation, accepted their call.

And you called me out of the pagandom of original sin into the Church—your modern chosen people—and into a life which bore strangely beautiful resemblance to your own. I long took baptism for granted. I have not been shocked when I have heard Catholics complain, "I did not ask for life; I did not ask for baptism; why am I bound by the laws which follow from both?" How could they miss and how could I be even briefly unappreciative of the call which brought us out of the natural into the supernatural, out of the life of flesh and spirit into the world of divine grace, out of the poverty of original sin into the infinite riches of sanctification?

It really seems a little sad that people keep waiting for their vocation. Children would be much happier if they early learned that they had been called by you into the family that is theirs, the home they shared, and their important profession of being good sons and daughters.

When I gave a reason for not doing something I did not want to do, my mother (heaven bless her) would say, "God wants you to do it." I used to wonder a little how you got into the situation. "God will be pleased if you do this" was not much different from "Mrs. Kelly will be pleased if you play your new piece for her on the piano." I wasn't sure that Mrs. Kelly would be overjoyed at my massacre of music, and that perhaps you wouldn't be too delighted if I performed some small task or completed some trifling chore.

Perhaps it is only with some spiritual maturity that one comes to know the lovely and inspiring truth, the truth that can transform one's whole attitude toward life, that every position we occupy is the result of a direct call from you. I was called upon by you to be a good little boy. I was given the vocation of being an obedient son. When first I went into primary grade, that too was your vocation to me. It was less the school bell than your voice which summoned me to class or the games of recess. Would the school boy move so reluctantly to school if he could hear your summoning voice?

Looking back, I am humbly happy that you called me constantly to happy places and the company of good people. When you asked me to study (in preparation for my work for you), you called me to a school with a pure and wholesome atmosphere. Would a juvenile delinquent have been possible in the environs of dear old Holy Angels? I find it hard to believe. Though we came from a section of town that had the two elements of peril, a district rapidly running down at the heel, sliding on its way to a slum, and the boulevard on which the newly rich were trying devotedly to spoil their children, all of us were extraordinarily good small boys and girls, and continued into sound and morally healthy adolescence.

You had called me to a fine Catholic home. My vocation as a young learner brought me the companionship of surprisingly sound youngsters. I can even recall our bewilderment when a rotten apple was dropped briefly into our pedagogical barrel. You must have swiftly scooped him out and delivered us from his contamination; for I remember him as a flash of rather frightening force and brevity in our school. Then he was gone and I have forgotten his features or his name or why his example repelled and fascinated us.

Life is a beautiful thing, dear Lord, when we see it as your constant call. It becomes a little like the life of a small boy whose devoted father makes him partner in all that interests him. "I'm working in the basement painting a chair, son; come and help me." "How about helping your mother and me clean up after dinner?" "It's time we dug up the garden, fella; don't you want to handle a shovel with me?" "I'm going to the store to pick up some hardware;

want to come along?" "That motor needs some overhauling, son; come on and let's work on it together."

Life becomes such a wonderful sharing when you see clearly that we both share it.

From the moment of conception, we have the most glorious vocation, for we are called to be your children and your partners in the conduct of the world. Nothing seems trivial when that basic foundation is laid. Nothing that we do seems even slightly unimportant or valueless. Yet though it is an inspiring fact, I had to know my major vocation before I came to realize and act on it.

May I pause once more, dear Lord, while I thank you for the great vocation of my life? Of the millions who would have served you better, you still called me to be your religious and your priest. I might try to stifle your voice with music and laughter and the tap of dancing feet and shouts and protests, but your voice came through. I might ignore you, pretend your voice was a mere ringing in my ears, but your call continued, you would not take No for an answer.

So, disliking your call and protesting I did not want it, I came in answer like some small, reluctant, bad boy . . . to priesthood and partnership with you in life's greatest profession. You were asking me, though I did not know it, to do Christ-like work. You must have known in advance how that Christ-like work would be done in a most un-Christ-like fashion; nonetheless you called me, wheedled me, threatened me, bribed me, almost forced me to come. Why? I shall never know.

Then during that first Long Retreat (which always rated the capital letters in which I think of it), you made clear what life could mean. You had called me to professional participation with you in the salvation and happiness of mankind. Of mankind, I was to be the most important unit. First I must be perfect as you are perfect and as your Son taught us to be perfect. The challenge should have appalled me. Actually, I hardly knew it was a challenge, for you were breaking truth to me in easy, unstartling stages. I was to practice the virtues to which you called me in the religious order to which I had been invited. I was invited to share the wisdom of the classics and the perceptions of the philosophers and the discoveries of the scientists and the art of the poets. I was invited into the laboratory where the science of the saints was taught and practiced and Christ, your Son, was the chief professor.

And ahead of me, for the happy lifetime to be mine, was comradeship with you in the glorious work for your world.

Dear Lord, I have been lucky indeed, for I have heard you calling me. My life has been a response, sometimes quick and sometimes laggard, occasionally with prompt delight but often with grumbling, reluctance, distaste, to your repeated invitations.

So all lives were meant to be, no matter what their vocation.

And if all lives were just this, all life would be incredibly useful, beautiful, rich in achievement, and the world would bloom like another Eden, or like that Heaven where your voice is the most sublime music.

I am grateful for the constant vocations that have been mine. I am ashamed of my too frequent deafness, hesitation, and protest. Speak, Lord, for your son and servant will try to hear.

Your obedient son,

IX

Dear Lord Jesus,

May I stand beside you when, the Eternal Word of God, you hesitated on the battlements of Heaven? I use the word "hesitate" in a purely human sense, of course, for there was surely no hesitation about your approach to the Incarnation. You gave yourself into that almost with precipitousness . . . "emptied yourself," St. Paul said, as if you were pouring water out of a pitcher.

Yet for my slow sake, I am asking you to pause for just a second, while I take my place beside you and try to understand that awesome decision that held you suspended between your eternity of perfect happiness in your Heaven and the thirty-three years of human life and then the centuries of continued presence among mankind on earth.

Thanks be, that imagination can destroy time and distance, or rather, create and recreate dates and places. For nineteen centuries and more have passed since that moment of Great Decision. All history will split itself into the time before and the time after this moment. "Before Christ," we will call the years that preceded; "the Years of our Lord" we call all days and hours and all time that has felt your presence.

Heaven is breathless, for this is the instant for which all other instants have waited. The faithful angels understand at long last your plan. If speculation about the Scriptures is true, the evil angels fell because they were shown a vision of what would happen after you arrived on earth: they saw the stable, the manger, and the Child; and hooted in indignation at the suggestion that they kneel and adore you. Now we can fancifully listen while faithful choirs of angels pause in the rehearsal of the hymn of the Nativity. Their "Gloria" fades away down the corridors of the heavenly practice hall, for they are watching what will now occur.

They see your heavenly Father bow his head in assent to the sacrifice you are about to make, and they are dumbfounded that some greater than ordinary miracle threatens to bury your divinity in the tiny fragment of humanity prepared for your Incarnation. The Holy Spirit broods over the unsuspecting Mary, his power ready to overshadow her. And there is silence, deep and expectant, through the palaces of Heaven and up and down the breathless streets.

I should surely seem out of place at your side at this peak moment, a pale shadow against your shining majesty, a thin nothing against your greatness. But no one would notice me. All Heaven has concentrated in undivided focus upon the one overwhelming fact—you, the Word of God, the timeless Son of the Father, the second Person of the Trinity, are about to make your way from eternity to time, from Heaven to earth, from the adored splendor of divinity to the humility of your manhood. You are still completely God; and soon you will be also one of those creatures who have so disrupted all the rest of creation on earth: you will be man.

I can see you turn your eyes back toward the Heaven you have known for all eternity. Once there was the perfect completeness which is the Holy and love-united Trinity. The Father and Holy Spirit with you, the Divine Son, had needed only the fullness of that threefold perfection. You had known complete content. Yet back in the unrecorded reaches of beginning time, you had determined to add to Heaven its complement of angels. You may have thought of that moment of shining creation now as you turn toward the salvation of a lesser creation.

Did you create the angels all in one single, soft-spoken "*fiat*"? When the Council of the Trinity had decided that angels should be created, did you speak the command, "Let there be angels of light!", and were they suddenly standing before you . . . each angel different from all the others, each shining like the yet uncreated stars and suns and whirling meteors, each turning to you in a first shout of homage and adoration? That would have been a beautiful spectacle and the possibilities intrigue me. A moment before, the streets of Heaven had been empty; now they are filled with the rushing flight of angelic messengers. The courts of your Heavenly Palace had been amply filled with your glorious presence. Now sentries stand at attention and processionals of singing angels move down the corridors. There is the whirr of wings and the whispers and cries of wonder as newly created angels see first themselves, then the Heaven into which they have been brought, and then, to their utter joy, you, their Creator and their God.

I find it fascinating to imagine a Heaven devoid of population, suddenly filled with angelic messengers and soldiers and singers and dancers and poets and scholars and courtiers, each unique, each glorious and happy.

It may have been, and some day you may tell me, that you created the angels a few at a time, beginning, perhaps, in a sort of heavenly evolution, with the lowest choirs. Each new creation might have been a lovelier level of angelic beauty and power and intelligence, until you came to the making of Lucifer himself, the topmost point of angelic creation, the Light-Bearer who made unnecessary the creation of a sun, and who, with time, was to regard himself as a possible rival for the glory of the Beatific Vision. Perhaps that too could be.

However that may be, looking back at the Heaven that waits on tip-toe for what you are about to do, you remember the rebellion that cut in half the population of Heaven. You never forgot (for you were to speak of it warningly to your disciples) how Lucifer fell like lightning from the clouds. He was like a sun tossed sharply from the sky. He fell in a great shower of his own beautiful sparks; and perhaps carried with him the flame that was to burn forever in Hell.

Yet even now as you hesitate between the perfect joy of Heaven and the confusion of earth, you might well have paused in divine surprise. Had you decreed to redeem the angels, you needed make no headlong flight through space. You could have redeemed them taking the nature of one of the more glorious spirits, these in your own heavenly city. Why you did not is beyond my guessing.

I am grateful that at that moment, although you know you are plunging into a sinful world, you also know you are entering the sinless body of the waiting Virgin. The soul of the human race may be yellow and cynical, wintry in its disbelief; but the soul of Mary that waits to embrace you is immaculate and warm with more than mother love. For that I am grateful as I am grateful for what you foresee of the loyalty of Joseph, the ministry of John the Baptist, the love of Mary Magdalene, and the quick first response of the disciples. But these are dubious compensation for what else you see.

If you have known choiring angels in Heaven, you will know contemptuous silence on earth. If angels have served you on flashing wings, men will not serve you at all, or grudgingly. If the courts of Heaven are crowded, the road to Bethlehem will be forsaken. If you are the delight of the heavenly Court, you will be the scandal of the courts of the Temple.

Midway between Heaven and earth, the Son of God hesitates. He is on the razor's edge between eternal happiness and the rigors of an earthly existence. He is surrounded by the angels for whom he is complete delight; he hovers over those men who will neglect and reject, hound him, and finally hang him to the cross.

Dear Lord Jesus, it must have been a moment of dreadful decision. You do not hesitate; but as in imagination I stand beside you, I hesitate for you. I simply cannot understand why you do what now you do. You accept the cross, despising the shame, and I watch and marvel that you do.

Of course, it could give me an exalted idea of my own importance.

For the decision is made with your eyes fixed on me. I was the tiny particle tossed into the scale that toppled you from Heaven and sent you hurtling down into space. My sin upset the universe; and now, in a fantastic sort of way, it upsets the God of the universe, transferring him voluntarily from bliss to labor, from peace to passion.

Let me take that downward flight with you, Lord Jesus. For I do not want to remain in Heaven if you are bound for earth. You are going to serve me and my fellow men. You will, if I permit you, bring Heaven to earth and into the life of

Your grateful son,

X

Dear Lord Jesus,

If I could stand at your side and see things with your eyes, if your hand would point to things worth seeing and persons worth watching, I'd be a very fortunate person, wouldn't I? You've made that possible in a good many ways, if I care to take my stand near you. And your words have indicated a lot of things, and your gesture has made clear some very baffling problems. But I fear I am too busy standing on my own feet and making my own decisions and seeing things with my own eyes to give you much opportunity.

But once more, if I may, I should like to stand beside you . . . at one of the definitive moments of your life.

You have just left your Mother's house with a finality that is almost frightening. With what single-mindedness you concentrate on the job to be done! How decisively you cut yourself off from anyone or anything which is not your Father's business!

You have mounted a hill and now stand looking out over the scene of your public life that stretches before you. In what must be a blend of divine vision and human wisdom, you take in the scene . . . the winding highways built by the Romans, now flowing with armies on the march, caravans lumbering toward the markets, wedding processions and funeral corteges, individuals and parties and families traveling in nomadic fashion. You can see the small market towns and the gossips gathered around the village wells. You can see newly built Tiberias (a flattering gesture from Herod to the Roman Emperor—when will the first small town be named for you?) and in the far distance the white and gold of Jerusalem . . . and under the distant horizon, Alexandria, city of commerce, and Corinth, university town, and Rome, the center of the world.

I can stand beside you now. It would have been wiser to ask you to let me stand there when the Devil took you up to the high mountain, for he too made a gesture that was compelling and spoke words that were frighteningly true. He placed before you, for the vantage of that mountain crest, all the kingdoms of the world and their glory, and made his promise, which, were he not a liar, he could have kept. "All these I will give you, for they are mine, if falling down you will adore me." Never were truer boasts made. The kingdoms of the world were his, and for a good many centuries he had been dealing them out. He had shuffled kings and queens. He had never failed to play his joker, the little lie that nobody noticed. He could brag about a world-wide domain and know that he was speaking the truth. And you knew it, too.

But I should be uncomfortable in the company of the Devil. You sometimes frighten me because I know my guilt. He always frightens me because he knows it more clearly than I do, and has for it none of the pity that you continue to display.

Rather I'd like to stand beside you as you look out upon the earth that is waiting for you but does not know it. What you see must appall you. What you see, I need to see for my own enlightenment, warning, and encouragement.

The Devil was right. It is his. He sits triumphantly on the pagan altars of the nations. Sometimes he is there himself, Molloch or Beelzebub. Sometimes he is represented by ugly symbols, the snake, the crocodile, even the buzzard and the ape. Sometimes he lets his place be taken by one of his favorite vices, lust in the person of a beautiful young woman, or drunkenness as the weaving old Silenus, or a shifty-eyed thief or a glib and eloquent liar.

Greed and trickery, two of his favorite serfs, had even slipped into the shadow of the Holy of Holies, where animals bellowed and squealed and baaed, and the cloth on the tables kept the false coins from betraying themselves with their failure to ring.

It was a proud day for the Devil when he deflected the natural impulse to reverence and adore from God himself.

The university towns served him well. He had juggled words until few could tell the difference between truth and its opposite. Where men had discovered the truth, it had not made them humble as truth was meant to do, but proud. It ceased to be God's truth and became by right of discovery their proud possession and exclusive right. The courtesan became the constant companion of the scholar as Plato set the example with his Phryne. Wisdom and knowledge became new reasons for despising those without education and tricking them out of the truth.

How the Devil must have loved the slave markets! Whatever line of trade or traffic others followed, the buying and selling of human flesh was his idea of good business. And it was a day when that particular brand of business was the world's largest. From the hill, Christ can see the twisting caravans of slaves bound together ankle to ankle as they moved from slave trader to slave owner. In the open market, one could buy a secretary, a butler, a steward for one's estate, a cook for the kitchen, a field hand or gardener, a partner for one's personal sin, or the cat's paw for one's legal crime. Christ from the hill sees all these and knows deep pity. As he stands there, he knows that pity which made his evangelist write of him, "Seeing the multitudes, he wept." Those are sad words, but what he saw were sad sights and painful scenes.

Standing beside you, Lord, I look over the bent backs of laborers and the bowed heads of weeping mothers. I look at chins lifted contemptuously and hands that wield a whip or hold a dagger or a club. I gaze with you into the disorderly recesses of the vast state-controlled brothels and watch drunken figures stumble down the streets. Hands are quick in trickery and tongues are skillful in deceit. I watch dishonesty smiling across a counter and honest employees debased to make cheap, shoddy, crooked goods.

Yet, though the big sins make it a dreadful world, I wonder if at that moment you are not more disturbed at the sight of what we might call—is the combination of words too inept?—magnificent waste. The temples are filled with priests who have still some faint belief in the false gods, and who, in the service of these silent idols and images of the Devil, perform the most exact and often beautiful rituals. The sacrifices are offered with exquisite care. The dances and processions follow an elaborate pattern. The temples themselves, built to honor the Enemy of mankind, his most destructive vices, or human vanity, are monuments to artistic skill and creative endeavor. What awful waste!

Nothing has ever been more carefully conceived, more exactly executed, and more elaborately detailed than the marching of armies and the movement of fleets. Even now as you watch from the hillside, you can see Rome deploying its legions with the skill of an expert chess-player. A thousand men will march as many miles to camp in a small province and by their presence intimidate a possibly restless population. The galleys of Rome will today move from one great port to another, with vast creaking of ropes against wood and tireless strokes of slave-driven oars. The port they left will be swollen with the money spent by the officers to replenish their supplies and by the men on shore leave. The port ahead is already stirring in anticipation of the fleet's arrival. The merchants are rubbing their hands as they set out their worthless souvenirs. The taverns are polishing their best metal goblets and tuning their stringed instruments. The wharves are stirring to expectant life.

Do you see, Lord, into the hampers and carefully roped bundles on the backs of the camels? Men have crossed the deserts to bring back in triumph the sweet-smelling bark of trees, the perfumed excrement from wild animals, the backs of turtles that will go into the back hair of beautiful women, metal dug from the earth with slavish groanings to weigh down the arms and encumber the hands of the wealthy. That gold and those precious stones are among the only nearly useless things you ever made, Lord; and yet they are the things for which men work hardest, for which women long from the depths of their beings, for which lives are wasted and blood is spilled. They are the glittering symbols of human waste.

But I turn my eyes from the world of sin and wastefulness to your gently smiling face. Can that smile hide so firm a purpose?

Can your gentle lips match that determined line of your jaw? Is the purpose in your eyes what I think it is?

Can you, Lord Jesus, possibly conquer that world of entrenched sin and diabolical genius, of habitual wastefulness and systematized greed, of slavery and devil worship and lust, for the Kingdom of your Father?

You smile at me in a blend of wistfulness and determination.

"I shall try," you answer. And then you add the words which inspire and frighten me: ". . . With your help."

Indeed and indeed you will try. Your public life is the story of a magnificent effort. You struck at sin with all the arts of human ingenuity, infinite justice, and divine mercy. Your own unrelentingly busy life, your concentration on first things first, your devotion to your Father's business, is your answer to human wastefulness. You wooed the sinner while you struck the sin. You were as fierce in your expulsion of demons as you were gentle in your welcome to the repentant children of men. You spoke as no man had ever spoken before; convincingly, you matched each parable with your own perfect practice, and illustrated every precept you taught with the example of your daily conduct.

You did the perfect job, Lord Jesus. As you walk down from the crest of the hill to begin your years of teaching and miracles, you enter upon history's most fascinating and flawless career.

But that interests me less at the moment than your added statement: "With your help." You will not depend for the overthrow of Satan upon your divine power, but upon your human power united with the loyalty of your followers. You will work miracles but you will trust more to mercy, your own mercy and the mercy of those who imitate your gentleness. Almost your first action will be to gather around you the larger group of disciples from whose tempered and tested ranks you will ultimately select your apostles.

You have left the messengers who are angels to select a new company of messengers who are men and women. You will not call upon the infinite power of the Trinity but upon the limited power of creatures. You will join to yourself in gracious partnership the wise and the illiterate, the brave and the craven, the old and the very young, men of lifelong innocence and women who had known satanic possession, men who will become great saints and men who will sell you out for a thin purse full of silver coins.

The most mysterious and the most gratifying thing about your public life is your unfailing trust and repeated confidence in us human beings. You walk away from your divine vision of man's sin and wastefulness to pick sinners and wastrels for your associates. You are carried by the Devil to look at the kingdom of the world, and then you establish your kingdom using the very same weak, imperfect material which had done so badly throughout history. You never despair of mankind. You never turn away in disgust from humanity. You trust your work to Peter who will cry out at the taunt of a maidservant that he never in all his life so much as saw you. You will give the teaching of the truth to Thomas who almost loses his own faith.

And as you turn to walk down to begin your public life, you turn first to me. "Will you come with me?" you ask. "Will you help me to do my work?"

I am astonished and abashed at your trust in me. After all my failures, as a member of the constantly failing human race and as the member most characterized by failures, you still invite me to partnership with you in your work.

The work you undertake must appall you as surely as it appalls me. But your trust in me is flattering and inspiring. I know I haven't measured up, not remotely. I know that, however miraculous your grace and your example, I shall not measure up. At least, as if I were signing my solemn terms of partnership, I shall sign this document with a description of the role I shall strive to fulfill, as

Your loyal and devoted partner in the Kingdom,

XI

Dear Lord Jesus,

From the time I was a very little child, I knew that everything was right "if you were near." Your presence was my guarantee of safety. No one could possibly hurt me if you were near. You were my strength and sanity, my promise of victory over evil, my very source of power and knowledge.

Today I am asking if I may always remain in your company for one important reason: I should like to see things always with your eyes. I should like to realize how very true it is that you are the perfect guide to life. And a present guide for today and now, who every moment and in each new event or sudden emergency can show me what I should see, point out what I should avoid, and make crystal-clear what is true and good, and separate them cleanly and sharply from what is false and evil.

At your side I stand and hope to stand, because that is the one vantage point from which the world becomes clear. Life as you see it is life as it really is and should be. The things you consider important are important. Problems that confuse me become amazingly simple from your point of view. And a single gesture of your hand says, "This is it," and it is.

Since you certainly laid down a minimum of laws, I wonder if you do not find our fascination with the law a little childlike. "Let's see, what's the law on this?" is our way of solving a problem. We won't find many laws in your gospel. In fact, we soon learned to call your answers to life "counsels," as if you advised rather than commanded, and offered an explanation where you hesitated to formulate a rule. Your hand seldom was lifted in a gesture of command; it usually rose to point to the lilies of the field or indicate the birds of the air or embrace in a wide circle the obedient world

71

that your Father had made. You did not point and cry, "Go!"; you stretched out your arms and seemed to draw mankind in to your warm influence as you said gently, "Come!" You were more likely to give a joyous explanation, "Blessed are the clean of heart!", than to issue a harsh mandate. Your two commandments were softened by the fact that both concerned "love." "Thou shalt," your words began, and mankind, accustomed to the thunder of the Law-giver, winced slightly; "thou shalt . . . love," you concluded, and all the rigor and fierceness disappeared from the new commandment.

A new commandment you gave us; and what a sweet thing it turned out to be; "A new commandment I give you, that you love one another as I have loved you." First you had given the example and then you formulated the commandment. First you proved how charming love could be, how healing and consoling and completely reassuring; and then you smiled and said, "That was my way of life; make it your way and life will be lovely."

The world grows discouraged with rules and laws, Lord Jesus. Never had races been so law-bound as the Jews and the Romans. The Jews had a law for every moment of their day, for every moment of the Sabbath, for precisely the weight of the grains of incense to be laid on the altar, for the exact length of the fringes they draped over their foreheads. The Romans mastered law where they couldn't master conduct. They knew all the rules and rubrics and lived personally lawless lives. They could move into a conquered people and bind them with highly complicated nets of laws; but they themselves imitated the immoral gods of Rome in their own free-wheeling lives.

The Pharisees knew all the rules of dignified conduct and nothing about mercy or gentleness. They could quote all kinds of exact regulations, but when you talked of the law of love they were shocked and baffled. They could long for the triumph of the law of God and exclude from the mercy of the Lord the publican and the sinner. They constantly attacked you for your apparent disregard of the law, and missed completely the fact that your conduct was the highest possible law and your example was creating new precedent that never needed to be frozen into the sterility of multiplied commandments.

So I would like to know the privilege of walking with you as I watch you and listen to you and observe your conduct. I can do that in the pages of your gospels. You had a way of cramming into the three decades of your life the epitomes of all human experience. You were yourself all professions. You mingled with every class and kind of humanity. You managed to distill into thirty-three years every essential human experience. You covered the treatment of basic problems not with new laws (man had already so many that he walked in a legal maze that left him confused and discouraged), but with a charming story. Some of the bigger problems, labor, for instance, or the treatment of women, you handled without a word. You lived as a laborer and treated women the way you wanted us to treat them. That was your law; the shining law of your personal example.

You did not engage in long discussions of law and conduct; your conduct shone for all to see. When you had done something, you formulated what you had done in one brief phrase. I recall the way you illustrated the importance of prayer; those nights with your Father on the hilltops; those lovely prayers that came forth fountain-clear and spontaneously on occasions like the raising of Lazarus and the Last Supper. Then you put your conduct into the simple rule, "Pray always," and illustrated what you meant in the perfect prayer that began, "Our Father . . ."

I am afraid that it is a human failing to look to the law instead of looking to the Lord. We love the making of rules almost as much as we practice their breaking. We find a deep satisfaction in laying down the law for the other chap at the very time when we are finding a thousand plausible reasons why the law doesn't bind us personally. It is convenient to be a law-maker because someone decided a long time ago that the law-maker is not bound by his own law. They weren't thinking of you, Lord, whose life was utterly perfect before you dared to present us with one of your gracious counsels or your inspiring beatitudes.

Well, all this is by way of saying that I think I know how life can be simply lived. In the pages of your story, you have left for those who read and run, or reading, run to imitate you, the perfect example of how you did things, and then the affectionately expressed analysis of what you did. I should pay much more attention to your conduct than even to your counsels. Conduct came first; counsels were almost like an afterthought for those who needed diagrams to understand your simple approach to life.

But beyond that, dear Lord, I must have you constantly with me to see the answer to today's question and this moment's problem. Most answers and solutions you gave long ago. Yet each situation seems to come with a new face, a fresh insistence on attention, and an air of startling uniqueness. What shall I say to this temptation? How shall I handle a tendency in myself that I just happened to notice . . . or some "kind friends" have taken the pains to point out?

I can, of course, rush to the law library and stand baffled in the midst of the shelves of law books, each paragraph of which briefly solves a problem which somehow manages to remain unsolved; each precedent in which answers once and for all a question that never really has been answered. I can run my hand through my hair and my finger down the tables of contents. I can study everything from the Talmud to the Law Digest, from the law of Hammurabi to the latest supplement to the Code of Canon Law . . . I can, that is, if I have nothing but time, a legal mind, and the ability to understand the million human factors that helped shape the ebb and flow of the legal tides.

Or I can stand beside you and ask, "What would you have done, dear Lord?"

I have not the slightest doubt how you would act where justice and mercy are involved. I have no hesitation about the fact that you would place people first and precepts second. I think I can hear your voice asking in every instance, "Are you following the law of love?" I am sure that you would make as your test, "Blessed are you if you . . ." The test of conduct would be the happiness that followed from it. I doubt if you would find a frown the answer. The sharp word, I am sure, would jar you. You would find it amazing how your followers could turn back to legalism when you had come to give them the liberty of the sons of God.

I somehow feel that you may give me the grace to read the answers to modern problems in your eyes. Certainly they would rest with approval on what we have done that is good, social legislation for instance, or hospitals, or our efforts to bind the world together into some sort of peaceful union.

Couldn't I rather easily imagine you taking my place as I face a problem and acting rightly . . . with perhaps the right words falling into a brief formula later on? The old painters who loved to dress you in the costumes of their period of history had a reverent and a right approach. They wanted you to see life as they saw it so that in turn they could see life as it appeared to you in the current year. I am no painter. Yet I can, whether or not I ask you to don briefly the outfits we wear nowadays, ask you to let me see your face today and answer for me today's questions and solve today's perplexities.

And I doubt if there would be much hesitation either in your conduct or the words by which you explained it to me. And I am quite sure that I would hear you without much effort on my part.

For human problems are basically endlessly repetitious and embarrassingly simple. The answers you gave to an audience almost twenty hundred years ago sound strangely modern today. The worst crimes and the most vicious criminals of today are tiresomely like the sinner with whom you dealt. And if you were merciful to the

prostitute and welcomed the publican, you were fierce in your lash-
ing of the hypocritical misleaders of the people, the merchants who
put up their stalls near the sanctuary and the lustful Herod who grew
fat on cruelty and the shame of women.

Love has never failed to be the one universal answer. But I like
to imagine you loving in our age that talks too much and so stupidly
about love, makes a philosophy of its caricature, and then rushes to
the camp of those who march under the banners of hate.

If we are gadget lovers, would you destroy our inventions or
use them for the advancement of your kingdom? Would you be
proud of our scientific achievement and use our discoveries and
inventions as the basis for new parables and up-to-the-moment comparisons and illustrations?

I think you would. I think you would smile at us a little pity-
ingly when we insist that our problems are greater than men have
ever known before, as we brag that our achievements are always just
about to bring a new heaven to an old and weary earth.

But I feel that your answer would always be . . . first to do.
Your conduct would now as then come long before your counsels.
You would be far less interested in formulating or enforcing a law
than in illustrating the mercy of God and winning people by justice
and gentleness and a service based on love.

What we all need, I especially, is a place at your side. I will
watch your eyes as they fall upon the scene today. I will follow your
gesture as you point out what you consider important. I will notice
how you treat those who fill my days. I will see what you do . . . and
then listen for what you say.

We speak of you as our Guide, dear Lord. But you are so much
else. You are the one who put Life above law, and Love above life. You
were not nearly so much the Law-giver as the one who exemplified
all the brightness and inner glow and freedom and richness of the
law well observed. You were the one who showed that the law is not

in the mind but in the heart; not in books but in personal conduct. You were the Ruler of the world, yet you reduced all rules to the simple rule of Love.

Let me see through your eyes and imitate the gestures of your hands, love those you love and pity those you pity, hate the things you hate, and overcome, not with force but with the power of your personal conduct, the evil of the world.

I am sincerely going to try to take my place at your side.

Your most willing partner in the Kingdom,

XII

Dear Lord Jesus,

Of course, my feelings can't possibly be my guide to yours. Probably nothing could be further away from your divine mind than my oblique and twisted mentality. My judgments are on the stupid side. And my evaluation of things . . . well, it's good that I have you to help me form them, or I would probably be always wrong.

Yet I am tempted today to judge your feelings by my own. I am asking myself, how do you feel . . . after nineteen hundred and some odd years of the Christian era? What's worse, how do you feel after three score and a half years of me?

And since, as I confess, this is my judgment, not yours, I'd say you must feel plenty discouraged. Plenty!

It's nineteen centuries and more since you completed your part of the work of our salvation by dying upon the cross, rising from the grave, and making the great gestures by which you established your Church. Had I (once more I speak, like St. Paul, with deliberate foolishness) been in your place then, I should have faced the future with complete confidence. You knew there was nothing you could have done that you failed to do. You said so actually during the course of those final hours before your death, when in a kind of trembling self-scrutiny, you looked back, measured the outpouring of pain and blood about to begin, worked the miracle and wonder of the Eucharist, and knew that time was running out and that you must leave nothing unaccomplished. But you could find nothing missing from your part in world redemption. It must have given you a human satisfaction to look back and say, with finality, "It is consummated . . . it is completely done . . . the work which my Father gave me to do is completely and perfectly accomplished."

Yes, one of your disciples would fail you completely; but in the end the other eleven would be your messengers to the world. And eleven successes out of twelve attempts is an excellent average.

You had promised that you would send the Holy Spirit to help us. Indeed, in vision you could see the glorious moment of Pentecost when the apostles, cowering in the upper room, yet brave enough not to take to the hills of Galilee, would hear the rush of wind, know the sudden light above their heads, feel the flow of warmth in their souls, and rise in the strength of the Comforter to go out for the magnificent triumph of their first public preaching.

You had done everything necessary. The Holy Spirit would, as if anticipating some human mistake, come to supply for possible apostolic defects. And the first burst of eloquence from your Church meant the frustration of your enemies, the conversion of thousands, and the return of men and women from all parts of the known world to carry the Good News to all the Empire.

From the depth of that desperate despondency before your passion, you must, like a man in a well, have seen the stars shining at the same time as the sun. It was a New World that opened. Christianity was the new and glorious law of love. You had taught it and lived it and would die for it. How could anyone resist your eloquence, your example, your martyr's death for truth? You had come to bring fire upon the earth and shortly the hearts and minds of men would be blazing.

Well, Lord, it is nineteen centuries later, and (once more I speak from my human ignorance and not your divine vision) were I you, I would be greatly disappointed.

The truth did not prevail. Love did not root out the weeds of hate. Sin was not destroyed. The priests led away from you your own beloved Chosen People. After martyring your saints, Rome accepted your religion in less than half-hearted fashion. The onrush of the early missionary zeal burned low, and the fact that there were vast pagan empires, China and India, for example, left contented stay-at-homes unmoved. The merchant might invade the East in search of spices, silks, jade, ivories; but very few followed their trails bringing the truth and the Eucharist.

I wonder if you are proud of the so-called Christian countries of the world? I don't quite see how you can be. Christian kings bore you slight enough resemblance, with saintly exceptions. Slavery did not disappear. War was still the major occupation of full-blooded men. Women still wept and children were still to know hunger and want. Heresies arose.

You had predicted that the enemy, much more active, it often seems, than your friends, would sow thistles and weeds in your wheat field. But you did not warn us that much of the world would be thistles and briars and wasteland.

You knew, of course, but how did you endure the knowledge that almost two thousand years after your redemption of the human race, three-fourths of the world would never have been told that they were redeemed? They would never have seen your cross lifted in victory over sin or tasted your body at Mass. As many would wade into the Ganges as into the waters of baptism.

I marvel that you had the courage to go through with the passion when you foresaw the course of history.

What do you think of us today, dear Lord?

Do you find the flame of our zeal a pallid light indeed, hardly strong enough to keep warm the faithful of a single parish? Has the light of the Holy Spirit become as flickering and anchored as the light of the tabernacle lamp? You cried out that all men were sons of our Father in Heaven. You must be appalled that after all the repetitions of that prayer of prayers the world is still divided by hatred and racial tension and prejudices and wars and exploitation.

It would be so easy and convenient to lump the blame down upon that satanic enemy and the men and women who give his cause such full devotion. I hate to confess it; but I sometimes think that you must envy Satan the labors and the loyalty of his followers. You said once that the children of darkness whom Satan possessed and controlled were wiser in that generation than the children of light. But you came to give light to the world. What happened then?

It must be pleasant to be among those apologists who can summarize world history and the constant failure of your cause in easy phrases: original sin continues its sway; the enemies of Christianity have power and wealth on their side; heresy, after all, can be cleverer than truth; remember the overwhelming might of pagandom in every age; yes, but our foes have been so relentless, so unscrupulous, so willing to resort to any trick or brutality against us; and remember, they have Lucifer, the Angel of Light, for their leader.

Small consolation to me in any of that. And I wonder if there is any consolation for you, Lord Jesus.

Original sin continues? Yes, and you won for us the grace necessary to overcome its consequences. The enemies of Christianity have power and wealth? Yes, just as they did in Rome when the Pope stole the throne out from under Caesar, and the eloquence of the doctors and the purity of the virgins and the zeal of the martyrs burned away a corrupt empire and won a world—or so it seemed—for you. Heresy is clever? But did St. Paul think that the Sophists could stand for a moment against the truth? Would those early Apologists have been distracted by wittiness and glittering words and cried out, "The screen of smoke obscures the truth of the Son of God"?

Pagandom has Lucifer? We have you, Christ Jesus, incomparable Teacher, unconquerable King, Incarnate Son of the eternal Father, Second Person of the Trinity.

Yes, I know, how in your own day the same forces beat you down and finally nailed you upon a cross. But didn't you in human fashion perhaps think that that was enough? What further triumph could be permitted them? Should they be able again and again throughout history to repeat the passion and re-establish the cross, not as a triumphant symbol but as the gibbet of your execution?

It is almost impossible for me to discuss this question with you. I want instead to ask innumerable questions. I am baffled . . . and deep down I keep asking, are you baffled, too, Lord?

For in the end, it seems to come to one dreadful conclusion: the failure of your friends. If Judas had not led the armed guards to the Garden, you might not have been captured. If Peter and the rest, instead of denying that they had ever seen you and running to hide in dark alleys and behind Mary's skirts, had rushed through the city which five days before had given you the triumph of Palm Sunday, a popular insurrection might have swept you onto the throne of Israel and begun a reign of peace on earth. If the priests had listened, or if Nicodemus and Joseph of Arimathea had spoken up boldly in the council chamber for you, told the others what they knew to be the truth and dared them to take a step against you, history would have been very different.

I know. The passion had to be. Your divine plan for our redemption had to be accomplished in the shedding of your blood. But I wish it could have been plotted by the pagan Romans and not by the priests of your true religion. I would prefer to see some callous or callow subaltern in Roman armor leading the guards into Gethsemane and not Judas and the priests and scribes of your law. It would be much more reassuring had the apostles died with you than to have had them live on in treason, denial, and cowardice until a miracle of the Holy Spirit gave them courage.

It has sometimes occurred to me that perhaps one reason why Christian women seem to shame us less than Christian men is because the women around you in life were loyal in death. They faced the crowds on Calvary, not caring who saw them there if only they could show you loyalty and faith and love. They set an example that the men in your company did not set to the future men of Christendom.

However all that may be, I hope you are forgiving of our failures. I strike my breast, perhaps I had better rest with that. You understand the failure of history. You understand why three-fourths of the human race still sit in the shadow of darkness. You can perhaps tell me some eternal day why the representatives of Christianity came to pagans with swords, guns, cheap beads, and trinkets, with greed and graft in their hearts. You can let me know why your religion of purity has debauched native peoples and taught them new ways of sin.

I should even ask why the seats of the mighty have become comfortable easy chairs, in which it is possible to sit, sighing a little over the sins of the world, instead of being kicked aside while their occupants strode out to teach the Good News to every creature.

Some time you must explain my failures to me, dear Lord, gently and with that unfailing patience which is yours. And then I shall ask you, "Are you more disappointed in me than in anyone that ever lived?"

In a way, disappointment must have been the hardest thing to suffer in your passion. For the Passion was brief. But disappointment is your reward from each generation of unfailing failure, from your listless friends, from allies who consort with the enemy.

For my part in this portion of your passion, my heartfelt regret. Pardon and tolerance I beg for

Your partner who fails you so often,

XIII

Recently I leafed through the pages devoted by a national weekly to the coral islands off the coast of Australia. The editors stated that to most people it was a completely unknown world. Even Australians seldom saw it. Their article, they said, was like opening a window upon a fresh and undiscovered vista. I turned the pages and looked at the pictures with mingled interest and frustration. Here was a whole section of the universe, your variegated universe, that I had never seen and about which I knew almost nothing. I found it weird and stimulating and altogether fascinating. Yet the vastness of this one small section of your earth frustrated me. If a man decided in early youth to devote himself exclusively to a study of one of those small coral islands, an atoll with a circumference of perhaps two miles, he would not live long enough to explore and catalogue more than a portion of its wonders. Each day he would be faced by new forms of life, new beauties of coral, new instances of life and death that he would long to understand. In the end, he would die knowing that he had fathomed only one or two of the island's secrets.

All of which, I suppose, is just proof of your infinity and my limitless curiosity.

I am grateful that you made me curious, dear Lord, and I am sorry that I am not more curious still. Perhaps when I slip from the confining limitations of my easily wearied body, curiosity will awaken in Heaven, and I and the rest of those lucky ones who reach Heaven (please, Lord, grant that I do) will never cease to wonder and never cease to explore.

Could Heaven be defined as the place where human curiosity will eternally be satisfied and never satiated?

Even that, as I write it, does not look complete: Heaven is the place where human curiosity will be eternally stimulated, always satisfied, and never satiated. I forgot to put in "stimulated." But certainly our curiosity will be stimulated in the presence of your infinite beauty and truth.

Yet what an amazing thing is human curiosity. I find myself going back to that little jewel which you set your jewelers of the sea to fashion under the tropical skies. Those little coral jewelers had no curiosity. They settled themselves down first on the outcroppings of some island, and then on the skeletons of their dead ancestors, content with that tiny spot in the sea.

Then comes the cruising ship of the scientist along the shore, with the poet for his companion and the sculptor for his assistant. Out comes the camera. They pry and they peer. On pads of paper, the scientist makes a thousand careful notes and another thousand speculative guesses. The poet finds himself trying to tell the incredible symbolism of that little coral, working silently, one among billions, and creating a world of exquisite beauty. The sculptor is making swift sketches. If only he could reproduce the perfection of design he finds here: if his lines were only as pure and the color of the marble as iridescent.

Human curiosity must certainly be one of your greatest gifts, dear Lord. In a way it seems to be a test of life or rather a test of one's aliveness. Parents are reassured by the curiosity of their new baby. "He notices," they brag as soon as his eyes in curiosity appear to follow their movements or the swinging toy. "He is dead," we know, when a man's eyes fix in a cold, disinterested stare. A teacher is baffled by the disinterest of a student who has "simply no curiosity." We find it hard to deal with people who have no interests. Advertising men exhaust their ingenuity in an effort to wake our curiosity and sharpen our interests. The difference between a person who seems totally alive and one completely inert is the extent and variety of their curiosity.

You were kind, dear Lord, when you gave your children their enormous curiosity. Though curiosity underlies all discovery and leads to all invention, it means much more than that. It is another promise of eternal happiness. It is an appetite you gave us and mean to satisfy. You do not mean to let me die with only the tiniest point in the inexhaustible universe tentatively explored. You did not create my capacity for knowing and the curiosity that drives me on and in the end plan to trick me with a small dribble of partial satisfaction.

All of that throws me forward to the days that will follow death.

Naturally I find myself looking back rather than forward, to the visible world I slightly know rather than to the future world about which I know very little. My curiosity will be stronger than ever, and I shall have unlimited opportunity and all eternity to satisfy it. As I confess, I find myself looking back now toward the world I know. I am curious about the earth itself. I have visited only a few square yards of it. I have not sailed the Seven Seas or visited exotic lands. I have not seen even a small number of the fascinating creatures of jungle and air and sea. I have been held back from conversation with other peoples by distance and the simple handicap of not knowing their language.

The interest of the modern in outer space, the desire of men to see what lies a few miles down in the seas, I do not share. I wish I knew, of course, the answers that they see. But I haven't the curiosity that makes the scientist invent a bathyscope or weary his eyes at the outlet of a telescope. I am not driven to dangerous wastelands or towards the pole as the explorer is; yet I wish I had their zest for seeking and the courage that drives them on.

Back of me lie the dim corridors of time. An occasional bright flash in the past has been brilliant enough to hold even my casual attention. How many billions of exciting people have lived! How many wonderful events have taken place! Who actually did invent the wheel? When and where was fire first used to roast a pig or temper iron or make a bright flame for sacrifice? I want to know. I have seen motion pictures that aimed at reproducing the forward sweep of Egypt's chariots. I thrilled to the pounding of the charging knights at Agincourt, and thrilled even more as the bowmen of England changed the course of history with the flights of their carefully aimed arrows. I have followed the historians as they tried to reconstruct Waterloo or Salamis or Thermopylae or Gettysburg. I have walked through the libraries and known, with a sense of utter futility, the impossibility of recapturing even a small section of the past recorded there. To have heard Socrates talk! To have been at the Globe Theater on the opening night of Hamlet! To have heard Homer as he strummed his bloomin' lyre! To have seen the unveiling of the bas-reliefs of the Acropolis! To have sat at a lecture of Aquinas! To have watched Michelangelo at work on "The Last Judgment"! To have sat in the tent of Richard the Lionhearted and hear him lay his plans for the reconquest of the Holy Land! But especially, to have heard the Sermon on the Mount!

My curiosity ranges instinctively in the human past. And I think further back towards the steps of divine creation. I should like to hear your divine command that shook the universe out of its inertia and set in process the wheels of creation. Dear Lord, when I get into that realm of possibilities, I find myself fired with curiosity. That is a strange expression, isn't it, "fired with curiosity"; but I can anticipate what it may mean when, on the verge of eternity, I look back and see with your eyes the wonderful story of the universe you created.

Actually I may be deep in the reaches of eternity before I so much as bother to turn back. For my curiosity will have you there before it, your glory, your truth, your inestimable beauty, and I shall find myself impelled forward to seek, to find, to know, to possess you, and in you all else.

That probably is the meaning of curiosity. That is possibly what Augustine meant by that most often repeated of all quotations: "Our hearts were made for you and they will not rest until they rest in you." I am not sure that "rest" is the right word. Will we be anxious to rest when we find ourselves in the presence of all you can give us? When the early Christians prayed that they might rest in peace, they were probably exhausted by the stress and strain of persecution, by flight from their foes, by labor in the salt mines and slavery at the oar. Rest was probably the thing which then and there most appealed to them, and eternal rest was precisely what they most desired.

I am afraid that is not what appeals to me. A brief rest, perhaps, after what have certainly not been the too strenuous labors of my life, and then there is much too much to see, to hear, to visit, to learn, to know, to love. My curiosity I shall take with me into eternity, like an inexhaustible reservoir that I have never been able to fill. And now I shall be faced with the glorious paradox, the exciting contradiction: my curiosity will range out into infinity, always satisfied and always hungry. If man never grows weary of a really beautiful painting or a lovely face, I shall have you, the source of all beauty, before me. If a glorious landscape, basically the same and yet ever changing, delights generations of nature lovers, I shall be face to face with the Creator for whom that landscape is a minor, incidental achievement.

The dear melody of a familiar tune is endlessly delightful and the new music wakes emotions never felt before. Here I shall have the familiar music of your voice and the exhaustless repertory of your wonders. A great story written into a book gives joy to millions. Here is the story of the Trinity, of creation, of redemption and sanctification, of divine love and divine mercy, of the ultimate victory of good over evil, and the triumph of truth over error, and it is mine to peruse, not with inaccurate and tiring eyes, but with the fresh powers of my awakened soul.

I find it hard to put all that I am feeling and thinking into words. But then, no one has even attempted to describe the moment when arriving in eternity the soul knows that the shell is broken, its limitations are dissolved, there will be sight without straining and sound without confusion and knowledge without effort and love without disillusion. And the great gift of curiosity, carried across the barriers of time, suddenly is presented with the untrammeled, unrestricted, completely possessed fact of infinity in eternity.

Well, the words are growing abstract and inadequate, dear Lord. I started out to thank you for the vital gift of curiosity. I wanted to tell you that I am glad you gave me much of that gift, and I regret that you did not give me even more; or, probably to put it more correctly, that you did not give me the energy and courage necessary to make it really an effective gift. I have not the curiosity of a great historian, a patient student of human character, a notable scientist, a theologian who dares even here and now to study and understand you.

But it gives me a thrill to know that what curiosity I have is hardly more than an appetizer for the eternity that lies ahead. What I have learned in my brief and limited life is a glimmer of what I shall know when, in your mercy, I have the boundless you in unlimited eternity.

Thanks for my curiosity. You would have been cruel indeed if, giving me this gift, you had not meant to satisfy it. But you do. That is the truly wonderful fact; you do. I shall be able to recapture from the past all that I missed. I shall be free of the chains of time and space. And all the future will be filled with you, infinite you. I'm just a little curious how I shall feel when curiosity glimpses what lies ahead of it in Heaven.

Your grateful son,

Daniel

XIV

Dear Lord,

Of course you've noticed one of our most familiar expressions. We start using it when we reach the age of consciousness; we never stop using it until . . . well, until it has no further earthly use. And then, I've just been thinking, we'll really start to use it right.

"Oh, now I see."

It's fun to hear a child say that. His parents have been patiently trying to explain something to him. He shakes his head. They don't seem to be getting anywhere. They can't understand how he almost refuses to understand. They've been using the simplest possible words, drawing him pictures on a piece of scrap paper, illustrating it with comparisons, but he shakes off their explanation the way a shaggy dog shakes water, and his eyes, under his puzzled little brow, are clouded, almost frustrated. Then, suddenly, to use another of our favorite expressions, "light dawns." His eyes are filled with the light of discovery; he claps his hands; he fairly bounces up and down with excitement. And oh, what an air of pride fills him! He has found a great truth, and forgetting all about his parents' patient explanation, he feels he has found it all by his smart little self. Then he gives forth his triumphant shout: "Oh, now I see!"

Any teacher who has stood in front of a class trying to make clear some essential point on which, perhaps, all that follows depends, knows the frustration and bewilderment that cloud the faces in front of him.

"Oh," the teacher protests, wanting to reach out and blast a few of those rockbound cliffs that pretend to be foreheads, "it's really very simple, and you've got to get it before we can move forward. Now let me explain it again." And he does so in the most transparent language he can find. Then a sharp sigh of relief runs through the class. He can feel the students settle back, happy and relaxed, as one voice expresses the feelings of all, "Oh, now I see."

Sometimes we say, "Now I understand," but that hasn't the same feel and conviction and strength of the word "see." When we see it, we've got it. Seeing is believing, the old truism runs. And the voice of the blind man is in a way voicing the text of humanity: "Lord, that I may see."

How often we stand beside a friend with a glorious landscape before us. On the far horizon, something fascinates us, and straining, we make out that it is . . . a distant windmill, a ship slipping in and out of the horizon, just the faint outlines of that famous mountain with its eternal snows, the ancient landmark about which all the guide-books write. You find it and you lift an eager hand to indicate it to your friend. He strains through squinted eyes. He puts his hand up to keep out the too bright sun. "Sorry," he says reluctantly, "I don't see it. Are you sure . . . ?" And then his whole figure seems to grow tense with excitement; the lagging drag of his words changes to a burst of recognition; his eyes focus sharply as he cries, "Oh, now I see."

And you both smile in contentment.

The sad part of our human experience, dear Lord, one of the many, many sad parts, is that we really see so little and see so badly. Nothing ever created or invented is more wonderful than the human eye. You did a beautiful job there, Lord, and with our cameras we've been trying to copy the perfection of your eye for a good many years. We haven't got too far, have we? But we keep on trying.

And as for those minds of ours, how badly they "see." It's our fault, Lord, for once again our minds are magnificent instruments. Wonderful as the eye is, the mind of man is far, far more wonderful still. Yet it is exasperating how bleary-eyed our minds become. We don't see friendship when it is offered to us. We see only the annoying little habits of a child and not the vast possibilities that are budding in him. We look at the world and never take in more than some small fragment of it. We see and promptly forget. And where your truth is concerned . . . oh, how badly we see it, how little attention we pay to it, how quickly we forget it, and how little of it remains printed upon the retina of our souls.

All this is prelude to something that just occurred to me. When death has come and gone and purgatory has blazed us clean, we shall, please your mercy, see the gates open and the light stream forth. I suppose, humanly speaking, it will be a moment of blinding vision. But it will be a strange sort of blinding, for as it blinds us it gives us sight. There stretched before us will be the glorious vistas of Heaven. Then, in all humility and gratitude, but with an assurance and relief and happiness for which all else has been mere suggestion, we shall probably say what we said so often in life:

"Oh, now I see."

Only for the first time we can use correctly the variant which sometimes we had incorrectly used on earth: "Oh, now I see everything."

If the truth be told, it would be more difficult in this world to get along without sight than without hearing. Or would it? I'm sure that is debatable. For when we pause to single out any of your gifts, each in turn seems to be supreme. At any rate, "seeing" has always been the gift most prized. For centuries, a really wise man was called a "seer"; he was someone who made a profession of seeing. To say of a person, "He sees things quickly," is to compliment his intelligence; to add, "He sees things clearly," is to be even more flattering.

So when the saints wrote or talked of Heaven, they apparently thought first of sight. Even in Heaven, they felt that things infinite and perfect would reach us through some equivalent of the senses. It was difficult to change our human way of thinking; and through the eye of the body, or the eye of the mind that is vision, all loveliness and truth and joy would first come. "We shall see him face to face!" cried out the Apostle, and of course he was thinking of the gracious foretaste of vision you had given him when he was rapt within the seventh heaven. You yourself in anticipation of the importance of the heavenly vision insisted that we keep our eye lightsome. The saints struggled for what they called contemplation, the human effort to see you clearly and truly and hold upon the canvas of the soul the picture of what they had perceived.

Yet this is such a struggle.

Then suddenly comes the glorious heavenly, beautiful Vision. And we cry out, "Oh, now I see!"

Like most important human words, "see" says too much and yet not enough. For in Heaven, we shall see you, so we are promised and you have guaranteed, as you see yourself. But it is "see" in that other wider, deeper, more reassuring sense of "understand."

I was thinking recently, dear Lord, of how hard I struggled to understand something of the mystery of the Trinity. My dear old saintly priest professor grew so excited when he tried to explain you to us that he verged on a breakdown. He seemed to strike out in frantic gestures at the words which simply would not make you clear. He broke open each successive thesis as if it were a vial filled with priceless perfume, as indeed it was and is. He grew so impatient with us when the mystery did not become as clear as it seemed to be to him. He drew diagrams on the board, diagrams that in a few lines of chalk tried to express the wonder and infinity that is you; and then looking at us over his shoulder, he would cry out hopefully, "See?" It was a question and a command, almost a prayer and a humble petition, a challenge and a dare—but I'm afraid we did not see and the mystery remained mysterious, for infinity was something that we could not understand, not even with the help of chalk.

But I learned enough about you to be able to pass an examination. I could talk of processions and relations as if I really knew what the words implied. But in the end . . .

Oh, you were God the Father and I could "see" what fatherhood would be like.

You were God the Son, and I could see, with the eyes of memory and imagination or through the work of the painters, your only-begotten Son.

Where the Holy Spirit was concerned, a dove and a tongue of flame were both beautiful symbols; but like the character in *Father Malachy's Miracle* (which must have had your high approval) I know that no one will ever draw a picture of the Divine Third Person that will make him clear.

The Trinity . . . that is out of the reach of my eyes or the grasp of my mind.

Then the eternal day will come when we stand looking down the beautifully foreshortened lines of Heaven's streets and corridors, and at the point of focus, we shall find waiting and radiant beyond all imagining: the Trinity.

Then we shall cry, "Oh, now I see," and beyond the need of study or reasoning, of thesis and syllogism, you will be there, complete and completely wonderful. And with the divine power which is your grace, we will see you as you see yourself, not "through a glass darkly," not struggling through the squinting eyes of our minds, but face to face . . . knowing as we are known.

For the first time the little verb "see" will really come into its own. For it will not be just the momentary flash of a glorious revelation upon the eyes of the soul; and calmly and contentedly, and with the growing perception that here is infinity and eternity to grasp it, we will understand.

Now I sit back and close my eyes, dear Lord, and say gently to myself, in a reassuring whisper, "Oh, soon I will see . . ."

Oh, dear Lord, make the Vision come true.

Your hopeful son,

XV

I suppose thinkers agree that humor is a human quality. Certainly
one cannot think of an angel as laughing, though there must be joy
in Heaven that is far more wonderful than our gayest mirth. As for
the devils, they are merely ridiculous (though hardly laughable). And
you, dear Lord . . .

Well, laughter usually results from the perception of the unexpected and incongruous. Surely you must see a great many things we
do that are utterly incongruous . . . the way we strut in our borrowed
brains and beauty as if they were our own, the vastness of our boasts
and the littleness of our accomplishments, the mountains of our
labors and the molehills we bring forth. But nothing is unexpected
with you. And when we know what is going to happen it doesn't
strike us as being funny. The joke whose point we know doesn't make
us laugh. The clown who slips (if he doesn't hurt himself) makes us
laugh; but we don't laugh if he keeps on falling because we know
he always falls.

Yet it seems to me that all around us are signs of a strangely
subtle humor that is yours. Or is it rather a kind of divine irony,
which undoubtedly you have?

"No," said my dignified doctor friend, "I never take a glass of
wine at noon; I don't want the smell on my breath."

There's an instance of your subtle humor; on the vine the
grapes have the most pleasing perfume; in the glass the wine has a
delightful bouquet; on the breath . . . not so good. In the same way,
onions are a wonderful addition to many a dish, but to them you
attached a kind of humorous penalty. And shall I mention garlic and
some of the rarer cheeses? There is a kind of ironic surtax on our use
of them that betrays us and plays tricks on our dignity.

I puzzle a bit over the fact that animal excrement is the fertilizer of our choicest fruits and vegetables, our sweetest-smelling flowers. And mushrooms, long one of our morsels, flourish in meadows spoiled by flocks of sheep or down in dark cellars where the sunlight cannot pierce.

You must have smiled a little when you heard a wise man say, "We become what we eat."

And there is irony in the fact that you ever bothered to create a thing like gold. Right now, aside from crowns for teeth and coverings for special service plates and rings for a bride and groom, it is one of the world's most useless minerals. Yet you ironically allowed the human race to think it vastly precious and to build up its whole system of barter and trade upon a foundation of gold. You must be divinely amused that we work so hard to dig it up from the deep mines in order to store it right back into the underground safety of Fort Knox. A man with a handful of gold on Broadway would be a king. A man with a barrel-full of gold on an isolated desert island would trade it all for hardtack, salt pork, and a cask of water.

You had an almost playful moment when you created precious stones and the gems and jewels that range through the earth in imitation of the stars. Yet what irony made you allow your sons and daughters to struggle for these so greedily? After you have a diamond, what can you do with it? Cut glass? What possible use has a ruby or an emerald? It can add weight to a finger and get in the way as a man plays the piano or pounds a typewriter. It can lie cold against the neck of a beauty and incline her to pierce her pretty ears to carry its weight. And yet somehow we think of them as being among the earth's most valuable treasures.

And are you a little amused at the way in which we try to copy your creations? You make a rose and it is completely beautiful; we copy a rose in our finest plastic and it misses the texture, the perfume, the thrill of life.

What irony made you arrange it that our mental wisdom and our physical strength come at different times in our lives? I have often wondered what we could do if our physical powers and our knowledge developed together so that we could when we reach the peak of our mental growth call upon the peak of our physical powers. Instead young athletes and old scholars are separated by a generation. The statesmen and the soldiers are twenty to thirty years apart. As man gets to the point where he knows how to do things well, he no longer has the strength to do them. Did you in a kind of divine irony arrange it that way?

Love works that way, too. It takes us human beings a long, long time to know how to be gentle with others, how to live with them in peace, how to understand temperaments and dispositions and fit our characters into the characters of others. Yet love comes very early when the boy and girl are completely green, rough and unfinished, immature, inconsiderate, and likely to bruise each other's character. If strength of love and strength of character blossomed at the same mature period of life, would marriages be happier? Or did you see a delicate comedy in two immature loves growing mature together, and gentleness developing to take the place of slightly frayed romance? Maybe you managed it so that we tend to love our fellow humans when we are young and coarse; and to find it easy to love you when we are old and, I hope, a bit refined.

A series of advertisements recently, I noticed, mention the fact that slow-moving things live long. It cites your amazing anticipation of the military tank. Is there something comic about our conviction that to get places we must rush, even if, once we get there, we are too tired to enjoy our destination, and realize that we have missed everything along the way? I suppose from the earliest days when Cain and Abel raced to see who could run the faster, we have loved speed. Aesop, one of your very wise pagan sons, laughed at the hare and copied the tortoise. But we still use speed to rush through the brief span of life that is ours, to go so fast that we miss your lovely world en route, and arrive all breathless and exhausted at even the destination which is the grave.

What gentle irony underlies the fact that from death life continuously springs. The honey comb in the mouth of the slain lion astounded your tragi-comic character, Samson. That the grave should be the most fertile spot in the countryside and that flowers bloom fairer and grasses wave more luxuriously when they draw their nourishment from the dead is something for philosophers to ponder.

In fact I think you had a bit of humor in mind when you made us so completely dependent upon the tiny world of hardly visible life. Man strides the earth, its master and its conqueror, but he eats because the worms and smaller, almost blind forms of life plough for him his fields.

Yes, Lord, I think you must have a real sense of the ironic and the ridiculous. But this I also know, you never laugh at us, your children, however foolish our blunders and however we may play the clown. You may use incongruity to keep us in our rightful place. You may show us the opportunities for laughing at ourselves. I believe that you even smile on us as a Father smiles upon a tumbling and absurdly clumsy little child. You encourage us to laugh at ourselves when we are in danger of becoming pompous or conceited. But you do not laugh at us even when we make ourselves ridiculous.

Let me have too deep a sense of humor ever to be proud. Let me know my absurdity before I act absurdly. Let me realize that when I am humble, I am most human, most truthful, and most worthy of your serious consideration.

I like it that creation is full of gentle irony. It helps me find and keep my right place in creation.

Your obedient son,

XVI

Dear Lord,

Your enemies and the enemies of the human race, dear Lord, have sneered at the profit motive. We never should do anything for the sake of the reward involved. We should never work for wages. We should do things because they are right, the things to do, a benefit to the human race, not because we would be paid for what we do.

Deep down in us you placed the instinct to think of the profit. Those who protest against it act on it all the time. They dream that once they have won through, in labor and danger and blood and lies, to success, they will be repaid in power, in peace, in personal comfort and prestige, in all the wages which are much more impelling than mere money. However, it was not of this that I meant to write. I merely feel this morning that it is very important for me to cling to a strong profit motive. I had better remember Heaven. I had better be convinced of the benefits that my personal goodness will bring to me and to the world around me.

For this is one of the days when I am sure that it will not be easy to be good.

Sometimes I try to persuade myself that goodness is really easy. And sometimes it is not too difficult. Sometimes I find that I can keep your commandments without strenuous efforts, for temptation fades, the inner pressures die down, I am strangely at peace with myself, and no prod seems to drive me on to evil. Temptation in any of its fascinating forms is surprisingly absent. Sometimes I can be good without a great deal of strain.

This is not one of the days.

Today I have no doubt about the fact that goodness is hard, virtue is much more difficult than vice, and that becoming a saint is just about the most strenuous career one could undertake.

So today I had better pause to think occasionally of Heaven and the glimpses of Heaven that come during life to those who can keep their eyes on their happy goal.

Just the other day, as I gave a retreat to a church full of university students, the difficulties of being good forced themselves in on me. Had I, with the assistance of your enemy the Devil, devoted those days to making those thousand young men completely evil, they would never have recovered from what I had done. In three days, I could have twisted their souls and harmed their bodies, turned them away from you, and set their feet on paths so evil and easy that their whole lives would know the effects of what I did. And I should not need to have been too eloquent, too convincing, too graphic in my descriptions.

I could with a few simple and really stupid arguments have done frightful damage to their faith.

Just a few hours of evil pictures, of well-told evil stories, of temptation paraded for their benefit, and I would have damaged their purity in savage fashion.

Dope can in three days become a nearly incurable habit.

It is so easy to pitch a man headlong on the road to hell.

But then, the retreat that I gave was being presented in a lovely Gothic church, and I realized how easy it would be to put the torch to it and watch it burn to the ground in total ruin. I knew something of the history of that beautiful church of yours, how an architect had traveled Europe selecting from a hundred and more churches details he would build into this new structure. It was a matter of years before he finally produced the satisfactory and acceptable plans. Then the church itself was two full generations in building. It was first just a covered basement where your worshippers knelt in semi-darkness. Then slowly and laboriously were lifted the forest of columns that sprout into the curve of arch and the richness of ceiling. The tall steeple that sprinkles the music of its bells over the city came thirty years later still. Only recently were the soft lights of the stained glass installed and the modern chandeliers added as a finishing touch.

Hold back the city's fire department, give me a good wind from the south, and I can burn that magnificent church of yours to the ground in a single night.

Rome, the old saw runs, wasn't built in a day. But it was destroyed in a single fierce assault of barbarians. Those crude villains couldn't have built a satisfactory hut for their dogs; but they could sack and ruin and then burn to the ground the palace of the Caesars.

You have a way, dear Lord, of making beautiful even the ruins which our hands create. I have always loved pictures of those ruined monasteries of England and Scotland. They were centuries in the process of formation; individual artists worked a lifetime to produce a single altar screen or the wood and stone carvings which emerged to give joy to the monks and the visitors. Then a single tyrant in search of metal for his swords and gold for his favorites' necks could gut those lovely houses of prayer and leave them for the bats and the field mice and the later sighs and regrets of artists and antiquarians. Only you with your merciful trumpet vines and morning glories and mosses and lichens could cover them over with a new and beautiful drapery and make them the dreamlike, lacy trellises they have now become.

It is so hard to build. It is so easy to destroy.

And that goes for a soul and a character and a disposition as it goes for a church and a city and a vast empire.

I suppose that it is part of fallen nature that it is so easy to fall. No one enjoys the exhausting climb to the top of the ski slide. Everyone able to remain erect is thrilled with the swift and exhilarating downward course. Who among us would be brave enough to walk a narrow plank across Niagara Falls? However terrifying the prospect, it would be the easiest thing in the world to let oneself go and fall into the rapids.

"Let yourself go!"

That phrase seems to express a very easy "out!" Let yourself go, young man. Why plunge into the tiresome years of study necessary to become a physician? Why bother with the patient hours of training and practice necessary to be a successful actor? Why master that politeness and good manners, that consideration for others, that understanding of another's disposition and needs, that gentleness and firmness, that cultivated love which grows from passion into reverence and affection, that careful training of children, which are necessary to make a happy family in a wholesome home?

Some strange barbaric instinct makes us love to destroy. The savage has such fun tearing at the canvas as he mutilates the masterpiece he could not possibly have painted. For years the lure that led men to battle was not merely a matter of loot, but the satisfaction they felt when they razed the wonderful city and saw it go up in a forest of red flame. Children sit on the floor complacently tearing the pages out of a beautiful book. Part of the thrill of the fox hunt was the death of the beautiful creature that is the fox and the thrill as the horses trampled down the farmer's grain and slapped the apples from the trees in his orchard.

All part of our fallen nature.

All part of that gesture which was preliminary to the ruin of Paradise.

All part of the curse, I suppose, which changed work from a joy into a labor, made it a spectacular thing to burn down a field of ripe grain which had been brought to near harvest by the sweat of men's brows.

I have sometimes puzzled over whether history-long admiration for the soldier lies in the fact that some soldiers heroically defended their countries, or that all soldiers are agents of spectacular destruction. We perversely admire the cannon for what it can do to blast the enemy. We build nothing with greater skill or relish than any weapon from a spear to a hydrogen bomb. Never is human ingenuity fired to such a pitch as when a war challenges it to produce better and more effective ways of blasting the enemy and his cities and all his works and achievements. Modern war has made a science of avoiding battle and aiming at the obliteration of the enemies' centers of life and industry. Just about the biggest single sum of money we ever pay for a sports event, we pay to the pugilist who in the heavyweight class batters another pugilist into insensibility. The sports writers constantly remind us that we don't like the skillful boxer nearly as much as the slugger. Even the TV wrestlers are trained to seem savage and give the impression of great battering power.

Even as, dear Lord, I write these lines I find myself interested in enumerating and describing the facts of human savagery.

No doubt about it, the stories of a great murder are repeated a hundred times as often as the stories of a splendid martyrdom. The labors of a quiet scientist may be appreciated in a vague sort of way; he seldom becomes a figure for our absorbed interest. The criminal can always gain our attention and make us pay him the tribute of endless scrutiny and analysis.

Yes, it is very, very easy to be bad and undoubtedly very hard to be good. Perhaps that is why you make the rewards of goodness eternal and infinite. Do you appreciate the difficulties we know? Do you see that it is much easier not to get out of bed than to rise early and get to work? You have that perfect love for yourself which unites the Trinity; but you must know how hard it is for us to pray. You surely see that character like water finds it easier to run downhill than to force itself up and up.

But today I know that goodness is difficult, very difficult.

I am tired, and when I am tired, temptation is a nuisance, not because it becomes violent but because I don't feel the energy to resist.

I should like to take it easy today; not to do the hard things which I should do if I am to carry on your work.

Holding back the unkind word is much tougher than spitting it out. I'd even know the satisfaction that comes when I've said something mean and clever and felt the recognition in the eyes of those who heard me say it. Today the flesh is heavy and I don't want to bother lifting it. There is work to be done in what we poetically call the garden of my soul, vices and evil inclinations to be rooted out, virtues to be cultivated. Frankly, I shudder at the effort involved.

Some days goodness has a great appeal. I wonder why that should be. Is it the outpouring of your grace? Is it a little respite from the constant labor of trying to build the virtuous soul? Is it part of the reward or just a little holiday?

But the fact is that today being good will be a long and laborious pull up a steep hill. It is a kind of holding action against the gay and gallant-appearing forces of evil. It is putting the shoulder under a heavy load and heaving painfully. Weeds grow too fast and flowers and grain much, much too slowly. Today one can understand the small child who pulls the chinaware for the sheer joy of hearing the crash. It would be fun to batter down a wall or watch flames crackle and explode. The tedious work of planning and blueprinting, of clearing ground and breaking a foundation, of laboriously piling bricks, and driving reluctant nails through stubborn wood . . . it all has no fascination today. To sit back and relax, to let the world drift its own stupid way, to listen to the anesthetic voice of the radio, and to permit the TV to exercise its hypnotic influence . . . that would be so easy and so extremely convenient.

Pardon me a moment, the newspaper has just arrived . . .

I am back, and once more I am apologizing. I have just glanced over the first page: the diplomats of the world have decided to call off their conference and that immediate struggle for peace. Planes crash in midair, and millions of dollars in equipment are destroyed in a flash of high octane gas. Autos crash head-on as they speed along a highway; lives are lost and the cars are complete wrecks. A boulder that was allowed to come loose over a highway crashes into a passing car. A policeman, weary in his work of protecting other people's property, turns burglar and is caught as he robs a store on his own beat. Two boys stand on a river bank while their chum sinks in the waters for the third time.

Now I am sorry and now, dear Lord, I do apologize.

It is easy to stand back and let fallen nature fall further still. It is simple to withdraw and leave the field to the enemy. Boulders crash with the easy pull of gravity, and a collision can in a flash wreck what genius invented and great labor brought into existence. And one slack day may throw back the development of a soul for years. It is hard to be good but it is the only thing worthwhile. I shall struggle even though I do not feel like struggling.

Let me remember that in return for labor there is the eternal rest of Heaven, and that the burdens are laid aside in the glory that dawns. Anyone can destroy. Anyone can coast. I shall not give in, dear Lord, not so long as I have your strength and your help.

Your devoted son,

Epilogue

Cancer Is My Friend

"It's cancer," said the doctor, "cancer of the lungs."

My question was inevitable. "How long will I live?"

They wanted to make it as easy as possible. And yet what could they say? "Who knows? There is no predicting with cancer."

I was relieved. I had expected to die some day of heart trouble, or a stroke, and I dreaded that sudden and perhaps sacrament-less death. Cancer seemed kindly, almost like the preliminary coming of the Angel of Death to say, "Not quite yet. You've got to do some thinking and praying and straightening out of life's ledgers." I had always, in the Litany of Saints, said with great feeling, "From a sudden and unprovided death, O Lord, deliver me."

I cannot but feel that the dread of cancer is greatly exaggerated. People with cancer often live long and sturdily. Cancer does not necessarily withdraw a man from his normal routine. Since we all must die, God is kindly when He sends a messenger in advance with a gentle but emphatic warning. Surely we can all use a little time to get ready for the Judgment.

For death is not the end but the beginning of the only life which can satisfy the restlessness, limitless, glorious cravings of our immortal souls. God permits disease as the prelude to death. If there should be pain, Christ bore pain first and shares it with divine generosity.

The realization that one has cancer sharpens one's whole outlook on life; the earth is more beautiful, the sky a little clearer, and every moment of the day precious, a thing to be hoarded.

I am glad that America is cancer conscious. But when I read that cancer is man's worst enemy, I am not so sure. I cannot quite understand the appalling fear of cancer. I have known so many who died gracefully from it: my priest friend who, with cancer of the tongue, went quietly to his room, spent months becoming a saint and died with a smile; the dean of a woman's college who ran the school from her bed, held interviews, pushed forward the college's development, and served almost better sick from cancer than in the full bloom of her health.

God seems to use the things we dread to draw us closer to Him. Since we must die and since death is really the entrance into life, I am personally glad that cancer, the kindly messenger, came quite a bit in advance. For life seems sweetest when it melts gently into the Life that is our Eternal Promise.

This article, written by Father Lord, was published on the day he died.

Daniel A. Lord, S.J. (1888–1955), was a prolific writer and talented musician and composer. Soon after his ordination in 1923, he was appointed director of the Jesuit-sponsored Sodality of the Blessed Virgin Mary. Under his leadership, the Sodality grew to have a presence in almost every Catholic school in the United States. Lord wrote regularly for the organization's magazine, *The Queens Work*. An accomplished pianist, he composed grand-scale musical dramas that involved hundreds of youth and were performed in different locations around the country. In 1927, Lord consulted for Cecil B. DeMille's production of the silent film *The King of Kings*. He worked with Martin Quigley to create the Motion Picture Production Code to ensure decency in film production, earning Lord the nickname "the Hollywood priest."

Lord wrote more than ninety books and three hundred pamphlets. His autobiography, *Played by Ear*, was published in 1959.

Rev. David J. Endres is codirector of field education and assistant professor of Church history and historical theology at The Athenaeum of Ohio. A priest of the Archdiocese of Cincinnati, he earned a doctorate from the School of Theology at The Catholic University of America in Washington, DC.

Rev. Michael Rossmann, S.J., is the editor-in-chief of *The Jesuit Post*. He joined the Jesuits in 2007 after graduating from the University of Notre Dame. He taught at Loyola High School in Dar es Salaam, Tanzania, and is currently studying theology at Boston College.

Thomas Gavin, S.J., was the author of Daniel Lord's biography, *A Champion of Youth*.